Staffordshire, Etruria, circa 1900. An original photograph by Harold Inkpen displaying the distinctive vistas of the potter's sides. Wedgwood Museum Trust.

1

UK GUIDE TO Industrial Heritage Sites & Museums

On The Trail
Of The
Industrial Revolution

Written & edited by Richard Mann

Gateway Books International

Contents

© 2003
Published by
Gateway Books International
Tel: 44-01202-759607
Email: gbmir@hotmail.com
ISBN 0-921333-63-3

You can use this book to discover the fascinating story of Britain's Industrial Revolution by visiting the places where it happened or which exemplify the technologies it created. At many of the sites you can even 'take part' by going down a coal mine, spinning in a 'Satanic Mill', riding in a canal boat, simulating driving a train and 'meeting' our forebears at Living Museums.

6

The Industrial Revolution Heritage Trail

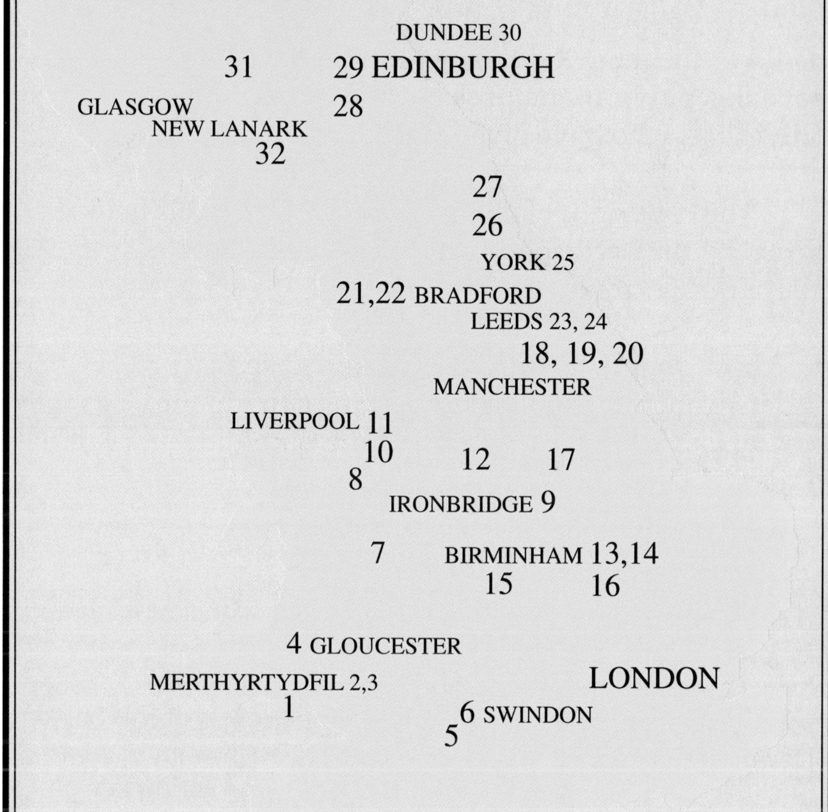

DUNDEE 30

31   29 EDINBURGH

GLASGOW   28
NEW LANARK
32

27

26

YORK 25

21,22 BRADFORD

LEEDS 23, 24

18, 19, 20

MANCHESTER

LIVERPOOL 11

10   12   17

8

IRONBRIDGE 9

7   BIRMINHAM 13,14

15   16

4 GLOUCESTER

MERTHYRTYDFIL 2,3   LONDON

1   6 SWINDON

5

Identify the heritage site number on the map
to find the location

7

A Word From The Publisher

To ensure that readers enjoy a high quality of information, the editorial content of this book has been reviewed and approved by the custodians at each heritage location.

The publishers would like to extend their sincere thanks to the many heritage museums which have helped make this publicatioon possible and to the scores of individuals who have given their support and time.

The copyright of all images included in this book is owned by the participating heritage sites unless otherwise specified.

Each chapter is fully self contained so that readers using the guide while touring can dip into it as they choose. Each chapter tells part of the unfolding story of the Industrial Revolution.

About Richard Mann

Richard Mann lives with his Indonesian wife between the New Forest and the spectacular seascapes of the Dorset heritage coast.

He once intended to become an archaeologist but instead followed a career as a journalist, author and publisher with a passion for history.

He hopes users of this book gain as much enjoyment as he did from visiting key locations from the Rhondda to New Lanark where Britain's Industrial Revolution took place.

Industrial Heritage Sites And Museums Help Us Experience A Revolution That Changed Our Lives Forever

The Industrial Revolution changed the way millions of people around the world lived and created the consumer society we enjoy today. It began in Britain because the conditions were right. At home population was rising and in 1760 Britain was already an old-established trading power as well as being among the freest and least regulated countries in the world. Men with good ideas and the skills to implement them saw huge new opportunities for making money. Indeed, if invention was the mother of necessity, opportunity was its father.

While it would be wrong to say that the British entirely monopolised inventions that led to or were part of the Industrial Revolution, a number of British discoveries and inventions *were* seminal and they way in which they were put to use *did* establish the framework of a new world economic order in which we continue to live today.

For example, the Italians had long been accustomed to clustering silk spinning machines in water powered mills and indeed it was from Italy that the design of Britain's first ever factory at Derby was copied (now gone except for the foundation arches). Yet it was the Englishman Richard Arkwright who invented the modern factory system of applying large numbers of machines to manufacture to achieve cheap mass production. He did for cotton spinning what Henry Ford would later do for motor cars.

Actually, Arkwright may well have taken a leaf out of the book of master potter Josiah Wedgwood whose contemporary ambition was to so much improve the techniques and conditions of pottery production that he could compete successfully with European and Chinese suppliers and aspire to becoming "potter to the universe." Pottery was one of Britain's most major industries in the 18th century and the entire evocative district around Stoke-on-Trent is still known as 'The Potteries.'

The Frenchman Cugnot experimented with the world's first locomotives in France in the 1760s but it would be Britons who succeeded in inventing and operating the first public railways. In the early 18th century, the Dutch had far more experience in financing industry and even trade than Britain but after their experts helped us set up the London stock market the City of London went on to become one of the largest financial centres in the world.

There is no argument that Abraham Darby was the first man in the world to discover how to smelt cast iron using coke, thereby opening the way for the development of the iron and later the steel industry which together became the foundation of the industrial world.

And there can be no doubt that it was the successive improvements to the steam engine made by the Scotsman, James Watt, which enabled the world to forever cut its ties with water and wind and achieve the awesome levels of power which enabled truly mass production. Contrary to historical myth, Watt did not invent the steam engine. This honour goes to Thomas Newcomen who invented the beam engine, a replica of which can be seen at the Black Country Living Museum, Dudley, close to where the engine was first put to use in the coal mines of Lord Dudley.

In Britain iron ore and coal were plentiful and relatively easy to extract. Roads were primitive but Britain was blessed by both by being an island and by having many navigable rivers. As the 18th century unfolded, to the seas and rivers were added the canal, that imaginative precursor of the railways which when they came would be the very embodiment of the Industrial Revolution utilizing iron, coal and the steam engine.

Today we are fortunate to be able to still visit the furnaces at Ironbridge where Darby used coke to smelt iron, a place so crucial for the development of modern industry that it has won the status of a World Heritage Site. We can visit the mills at Cromford, Derbyshire, which caused Arkwright to be given the title "Father of the Factory System" and Soho House in Birmingham where James Watt and his partner Samuel Boulton discussed how they would bring steam power to the world, manufacturing the engines at Boulton's nearby Soho Works. One of their engines still survives at Crofton Pumping Station.

We can visit the first canal at Worsley, near Manchester and the site of the world's first public railway which ran between Stockton & Darlington. We can even see where some of the world's most famous locomotives were made at the Timothy Hackworth Museum at nearby Shildon.

Iron and steel would have been nothing without coal and at Blaenavon in South Wales, conserved now as a World Heritage Site, we can see the world's first integrated ironworks and coal mines, the iron and coal shipped out initially by canal and subsequently by railway.

During the Industrial Revolution the rapid growth of new industries and towns like Manchester, Bradford, Leeds and Birmingham created horrendous social problems. So-called model workers villages were sometimes developed to provide better conditions and two examples of these at New Lanark in Scotland and at Saltaire near Bradford have also been designated as World Heritage Sites.

The history of the great ships that carried Britain's trade around the world can be traced at the Scottish Maritime Museum near Glasgow and even the history of the humble sack and bale in which the goods were carried can be studied at Dundee's Verdant Mill.

Ports and packaging were at the periphery of the Workshop of the World, the name by which Britain came to be known during its 19th century heyday when to industrial pre-eminence was added the largest empire the world has known.

At its heart were cities like Manchester, Bradford, Sheffield, Birmingham and Leeds, not to mention the great imperial capital, London. We can still get a sense of what it was like to work at the very heart of the Workshop of the World by visiting the Jewellery Quarter in Birmingham or the Cultural Industries Quarter in Sheffield. Here in red brick buildings, beneath belching smoke stacks, thousands of little masters toiled to manufacture the millions of small items which today we call consumer goods.

This book tells the incredible story of the Industrial Revolution by reference to the places where the history was actually made or sites and museums which exemplify it. There are scores of excellent and interesting industrial heritage museums around Britain but for those who want to follow in the footsteps of the world's very first captains of industry we hope that our industrial heritage trail will be useful.

It begins in South Wales, once the coal and iron centre of the world. In the early 18th century the River Severn was the trade highway of Britain's first empire and our trail winds through the historic port of Gloucester to Ironbridge. Here it turns south following the line of the Trent to Birmingham and then north again through the Derwent Valley Heritage Corridor. The trail circles through Lancashire and Yorkshire and then heads north via the National Railway Museum at York to Darlington and Shildon before looping through Central Scotland from Dundee to New Lanark.

For those who want to really savour the atmosphere of early industrial Britain a trip along Britain's thousands of miles of canals is more possible than ever and a number of key British Waterways and British Waterways Trust sites are highlighted.

Richard Mann

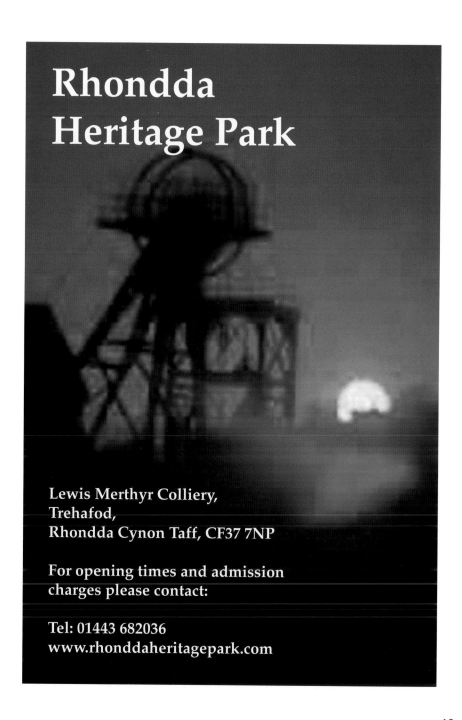

Rhondda Heritage Park

Lewis Merthyr Colliery,
Trehafod,
Rhondda Cynon Taff, CF37 7NP

For opening times and admission
charges please contact:

Tel: 01443 682036
www.rhonddaheritagepark.com

The Rhondda Heritage Park is dramatically and truculently unlike any other former coal mine in Britain. It is an experience. Multi-media displays sweep the visitor back to the times when coal was king in the Rhondda Valley. Real miners tell the real history of the real Rhondda in such a way that we can easily imagine we were there. In a way we are there. Visitors descend into a full scale representation of a coal mine at the former Lewis Merthyr Colliery by a cage the miners once used; below ground they see mocked-up sights typical of the miners' day and of the dangers he faced. The ride back to the surface in a 'coal dram' is as nerve tingling as a roller coaster ride as the 'dram' soars and dips at high speed through the narrow subterranean tunnels. Rhondda Heritage Park is so exciting that it makes you want to go there again.

Yet never for a moment is the true purpose of the Heritage Park forgotten. The purpose is to tell the modern visitor and generations yet to come not only about the mining of coal but about the lives of the entire communities the industry created.

The name Rhondda is often quoted as being synonymous with that of coal. However, just over a century and a half ago the Rhondda Valleys were almost unknown and existed as a sparsely populated rural domain. For centuries the Rhondda Valleys remained in pastoral glory, with clear running streams and waterfalls, and beautiful trees and flora. The small, sheep-rearing community that populated the few scattered farm houses existed as they had for centuries, as a sleepy rural community.

But then, in the second half of the 19th century came coal; King Coal, the black gold. Life in the Rhondda was transformed.

Although work was plentiful, in the early years working conditions and pay were poor and disastrous. The cramped towns that mushroomed on the back of the coal boom had bad sanitation which led to ill health, poverty and death. Rhondda suffered excruciating, hard and difficult times. Between 1868 and 1919 statistics show that a miner was killed every six

hours and injured every two minutes. As a result of these conditions South Wales was at the forefront of political strife as the militant South Wales miners sought to ensure acceptable living and working conditions. One Rhondda man, A. J. Cook, became general secretary of the miners' trade union and led them during the struggles and hardship of the General Strike of 1926.

A deep sense of this social past engulfs the visitor from the moment of arrival at Rhondda Heritage Park. At the entrance we pass through a facsimile high street lined with shops as they would have been in times past - even down to the contents of the original window displays. There is a glimpse into life in Rhondda Valley homes at the turn of the 20th century where miners and their families lived with a tin bath to wash in, an iron bed to sleep in and a loo at the end of the garden. The contents and fittings of a typical two up and two down terrace house has been reconstructed in the museum complete with crowded mantlepiece and a glowing fire.

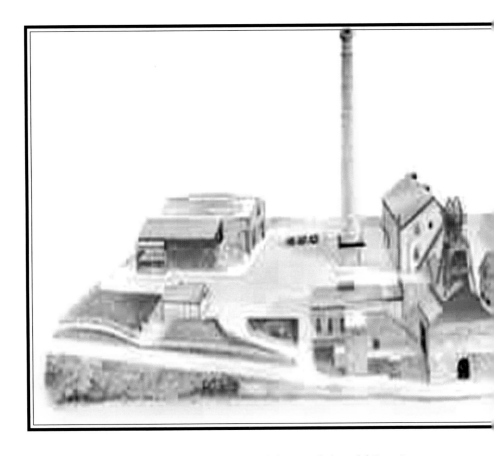

Two of the pit head buildings of the old Lewis
Merthyr Colliery have been specially preserved. In the Trefor
Winding House Bryn Rees tells dramatically the experiences of
three generations of his family working in the mines. Always
lively and evocative, you join Bryn in the middle of a working
shift and he reminiscences about life in a colliery as the huge
winding engine turns throughout this exciting show.

In the Bertie Winding House, Bryn introduces you
to Thomas, his grandfather. Exciting and fast moving
multi-media displays portray dramatic events in Rhondda's
history from mining disasters to riots and the fight for the
minimum wage in 1920. Visitors experience what it was like to

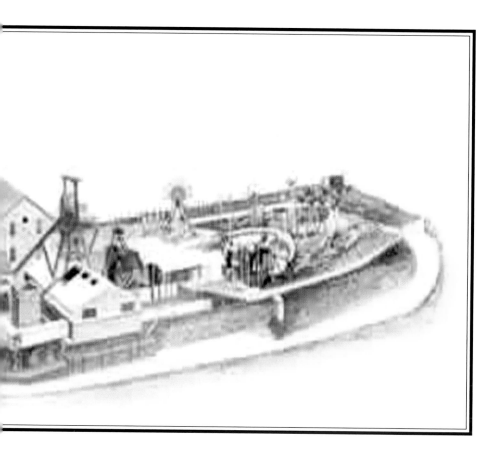

live in the vibrant valley communities during the hey day of the coal industry.

The role of women in the mining community and the cultural and social heritage of the valleys are colourfully and poignantly portrayed in the Fan House exhibition. The famous choirs and brass bands, the chapels and carnivals are all brought vividly back to life.

The Lamp Room prepares you for a 'shift' in the safest but most exhilarating colliery in South Wales. The Lamp Room is crammed with helmets and lamps and looks as if the real miners have just stepped out. After two minutes in an iron cage you arrive at the pit bottom - as it was in the 1950s.

All your senses will be working overtime down here and you soon appreciate the dangers, hardships and joys of working underground. You can touch the machinery, hear the effects as explosives are detonated, smell (and almost taste) the changing atmospheric conditions and humidity and see the shadows of men hard at work at the coal face. As in the winding houses, these underground displays, assisted by realistic sound effects are high theatre - but very effective for all that.

Nothing prepares the visitor for the ride back to the surface. Steeped in the conditions of underground working and now yourself below ground where imaginations can run riot, you board a simulated dram ride where you are hurtled and catapaulted through dark and twisting tunnels back to the surface. Amazing!

Rhondda Heritage Park has its own superb restaurant and picnic area but there is also an art gallery which exhibits the work of award winning artists as well as a souvenir shop selling everything from genuine

miners lamps to statuettes of miners carved in coal. If the children want to let off steam there is 'The Energy Zone,' an amazing adventure playground where they can climb, slide and swing.

The Bertie

Trehafod, Nr. Porth,
Rhondda-Cynon-Taff, CF37 2NW.
Tel/fax: 01443 688204.

An amazing 100 yards from the Rhondda Heritage Park in the heart of the South Wales Valleys. A well furnished bar and restaurant guarantees a convenient and comfortable stay at this recently refurbished guest house. Regular evening entertainment available.

Llechwen Hall Hotel

Llanfabon,
Nr. Pontypridd,
Mid-Glamorgan
CF37 4HP

Tel: 01443-742050 Fax: 01443-742189
Email: Llechwen@AOL.COM
Historic Country House Hotel minutes away from the Rhondda Heritage Park but high on a hill overlooking absolutely the finest views over the famous Rhondda Valley. A 17th century Welsh long house with a Victorian frontage, Llechwen Hall is a haven of comfort and fine dining. whether for tourists, business guests or special parties. On the threshold of the Brecon Beacons but only 20 munites from Cardiff, one of the liveliest capital cities in Europe.

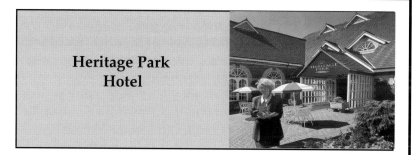

Heritage Park Hotel

As its name perhaps suggests, this hotel is located with amazing convenience right next door to Rhondda Heritage Park. And for those cautious about the kind of hotel accomodation available in the Valley towns, the modern and luxurious Heritage Park Hotel is an oasis of Welsh culture and comfort. En suite rooms, a la carte dining, well stocked bar and a traditionally warm Welsh welcome await visitors to the next door Heritage Park.

Coed Cae Road, Trehafod, Nr. Pontypridd, Rhondda-Cynon-Taff CF37 2NP
Tel: 01443 687057 Fax: 01443 687060. Email: heritageparkhotel@talk21.com
Website: www.heritatgeparkhotel.co.uk

CYFARTHFA CASTLE

Home to one of the world's most famous ironmasters

S tanding commandingly in its grand 160 acre park, Cyfarthfa Castle at Merthyr Tydfil some how exemplifies the way in which we imagine early successful captains of industry lived.

This alone might be sufficient to lure many people to visit the early 19th century home of the Crawshays, one of the most prominent iron-making families in Britain 200 years ago.

Today, ordinary people have a chance to enter the once exclusive portals and delve into every nook and cranny of the imposing house. But it is not only a glimpse of the way of life of the once famous Crawshays that a visit to the Castle reveals.

When you begin your tour in the old family wine cellars, you stroll past displays illustrating 3000 years of the history of Merthyr Tydfil, embracing the development of iron making in the town and its social repercussions and upheavals, including the Merthyr Rising of 1831. There is a reconstructed iron worker's cottage and even a reconstructed coal mine because after iron in the 1870s it was coal that kept Merthyr Tydfil in business.

Nearby, at Chapel Row, are superb examples of cottages built for the more skilled workers at Cyfarthfa Ironworks. Number 4 was the birthplace of Dr. Joseph Parry, probably Wales' best known musician and composer.

The 1851 Census shows five lodgers and seven members of the Parry family living in the two up and two down at No 4. The ground floor rooms are presented as at the 1840s when Joseph lived there. Upstairs are two exhibitions, one on Dr. Parry's life and the other an exhibition of the local choirs and bands that carry on Merthyr Tydfil's rich musical heritage.

The Crawshay family made its fortune out of iron, reflecting one of the major developments of the industrial revolution. Their portraits still hang in the great room where the family and their guests used to dine in luxury and style with food and empty trays fetched and carried by uniformed servants from the kitchens below.

Iron making began in

Richard Crawshay was responsible for the success of Cyfarthfa Ironworks

Inside Joseph Parry's living room

The Crawshay's dining room now houses family memorabilia

Merthyr Tydfil as early as the 16th century, but large scale production began only in the 1750s following the gradual adoption of the use of coke instead of charcoal in the iron making process.

Merthyr Tydfil and the South Wales valleys had huge quantities of coal not to mention the limestone and ironstone needed for the blast furnaces. In the years before steam, water from the Taff Fawr and Taff Fechan could be tapped for power.

By 1851 Merthyr Tydfil was established as one of the most major iron making centres in the world turning an obscure Welsh village of around forty houses into a noisy, bustling town of nearly 50,000 people within 100 years.

The first coke-fired furnace appeared in 1757 and numbers increased steadily. The best located was the Cyfartha Ironworks, parts of which you can still see today from the Castle steps. Cyfartha alone possessed seven furnaces linked to iron mines, collieries, limestone quarries, kilns and all the requisite trades. Six of the seven blast furnaces are still standing today.

Sometime around 1870, one of the furnaces collapsed or was demolished. It was replaced by a large arch to provide stability to the adjoining furnaces, still visible today.

The furnaces were connected by a system of tramways and bridges of which evidence can also still be seen.

Very close to the furnaces is Pont-y-Cafnau bridge, the oldest surviving iron railway bridge in the world. It was built in 1792 for the tramroad carrying lime from the Gurnos quarry to Cyfarthfa. In addition, it originally carried two water troughs, one above and one below the main structure. Cast iron was a new material at the time and, like the famous bridge at Ironbridge in Shropshire, Crawshay's most talented engineer, Watkin George, used carpentry techniques in the construction of Merthyr's iron bridge.

The works was first established in 1765 by Anthony Bacon from Cumberland but twenty years later was acquired by Yorkshireman, Richard Crawshay.

Crawshay, in many ways, typified the early captains of industry who brought about the Industrial Revolution.

That he ran away from home at the age of 16 says a lot about him. Selling his pony, this son of a Yorkshire farmer used the money to get to London and find employment at an iron warehouse. An odd choice, one might think, but this was the time of iron mania when industrialists were seeking to make anything and everything from this versatile and highly profitable new material.

Crawshay was a smart young man. He recognised the opportunities, worked hard and eventually took over the management of the firm. Over the next 20 years Crawshay's business along the Thames grew to be one of the largest iron merchant houses in the capital.

During this time, he worked closely with Bacon, soon becoming a business partner and moving to Merthyr Tydfil.

Richard Crawshay used his knowledge of the industry and his business acumen to expand Cyfarthfa, building an extension to the works at nearby Ynysfach and making Cyfarthfa the biggest iron works in the world. He pushed continually for improvements in the iron making process.

Crawshay also raised capital to build what became known as the Glamorganshire Canal so that iron products made at Cyfarthfa could be shipped more easily down to Cardiff and from thence to the markets of the world.

Eventually, the railways of Europe, the Americas and India bought rails from Merthyr and many a shot fired from a British cannon originated here.

By the late 18th century water power for driving the blast furnace bellows had been supplanted by steam with Richard Trevithick among the experimenters. Trevithick was not interested in driving bellows so much as in driving trains and in 1804 one of his locomotives hauled iron from Pen-y-darren Ironworks to Abercynon, thus becoming the first steam locomotive ever to run on rails - years ahead of George Stephenson and the Stockton and Darlington Railway which opened in 1825. The story of Trevithick's locomotive is told in the Museum and the tunnel through which the line past

Ynysfach Engine House

The art work to commemorate Trevithick's steam engine

24

can still be visited close to Cyfarthfa Castle. (En route, visitors can see the Ynysfach Engine House.) A major artwork has been created at the entrance to the tunnel to mark the event.

Richard Crawshay died in 1810 and his son, William Crawshay I worked from London. It was Richard's grandson, William Crawshay II who, against his father's wishes, lavished £30,000 in building Cyfarthfa Castle in 1825 at a time when iron was king. You can still see the office where he received reports and gave orders. From the window, he could keep an eye on the works across the park in the town below. Today, the walls exhibit a collection of watercolours, including early illustrations of the ironworks as it was long ago.

Cyfarthfa Castle is now also home to a fascinating collection of family memorobilia, fine and decorative art and curios brought back to Britain by early travellers from exotic and far flung places.

OPEN ALL YEAR

Part of the Castle's exciting social and industrial history galleries

You can also visit: Ynysfach Engine House Trevithick's Tunnel and Joseph Parry's birthplace

Above: Joseph Parry's birthplace

Brecon Road, Merthyr Tydfil CF47 8RE For further information please call: Tel: 01685723112

Blaenavon World Heritage Site

© Blorenge Books

For visitors to the Blaenavon landscape today, the high moors, dotted with slag heaps and pitted and sculpted by centuries of industrial activity, remain as remote and desolate as they must have seemed when the first truly modern industrialists arrived over 200 years ago to establish an iron works which aimed to be at the cutting edge of technology.

Blaenavon tells the tale of the formative years of the industrial revolution and is a cultural site recognised by the United Nations Education and Science Organisation (UNESCO) as being of "outstanding universal value."

Today there is almost something ghostly about the landscape workings, the old ironworks and even the town which history has now so clearly passed by as the traditional industries faltered and faded away. The shouts of workers, the clanging of iron, the rumble of tram wheels and the red glow from the furnaces and the coke heaps at night can now only be imagined

But the modern visitor's imagination is aided by explanatory displays and extensive renovations taking place following UNESCO'S recognition of Blaenavon as an exemplar of the industrial revolution and its designation as World Heritage Site.

NEW SOLUTION

During the 18th century, one invention led to another, each need to a new solution. Nothing was more fundamental to this process than the use of steam to drive equipment and to provide the "blast" for furnaces. Blaenavon took advantage of the new steam engines to develop a site which was rich in coal and in iron ore. It took only the ability to use coke to smelt iron to start a rush to South Wales for its coal and iron.

Iron had traditionally been smelted using charcoal but after Abraham Darby first smelted iron with coke in Shropshire in 1709, a movement of ironmasters from forest areas already suffering serious depletion to South Wales and even to Scotland got under way in earnest.

© Cadw

Casting sheds in front of the old blast furnaces

      The cheapness of coke smelting dramatically extended the range of cast iron articles manufactured. The exuberance felt at this can be seen in the many cast iron articles at St. Peter's Church, Blaenavon, including even the window frames, structural columns, the font and even gravestone covers.

South Wales possessed some of the largest iron and coal reserves in Britain and it was inevitable that 18th century ironmasters should choose to locate there. The mountains around Blaenavon also contained the limestone essential for iron making and there was plenty of water. All the requisites of coke-smelted iron making were handily available at this location, high in the Brecon Beacons National Park.

Ironstone for furnaces at Pontypool had been dug in the area for many years and when newcomers rode across the bleak moors in 1787 it was not with the aim of discovering or verifying resources so much as negotiating a lease for an extensive resource-rich site. Very soon it became apparent that the availability of coal, limestone and iron made the area ideal for the location of a new ironworks at a time when iron was very much in the ascendant. Whether for buildings or bridges, ships canon or tools, iron was in demand and big business.

IRON PRODUCING CENTRE FOR THE WORLD

South Wales soon became the major iron producing centre for the world and industrial communities developed rapidly in the otherwise rural landscape.

The men who began Blaenavon's industrial saga were Benjamin Pratt, Thomas Hopkins and Thomas Hill, all from the English West Midlands. Either as a result of personal or family involvement or though banking activities the three were involved in the bottle glass and fireclay industries, furnaces and canal building.

The trio were successful businessmen, fascinated by the new possibilities but perhaps also realising that because of the cap on interest rates imposed by Usury Acts of the time, reinvestment in the burgeoning new industries was the best way to make money. For whatever reason, The three were clearly very open to pursuing the exciting new opportunities of the time.

From the outset, the partners decided to use the new steam technology perfected in the 1760s by James Watt and in wide use by the 1780s as it was developed by Watt and his

Workers' homes at Stack Square which now includes an informative permanent exhibition describing the Ironworks and the surrounding landscape

partner Matthew Boulton at Soho Works. Unlike the water wheels which were used to drive the bellows which produced the blast of air needed to blow the old charcoal furnaces, steam could be used to blow several furnaces at once and Blaenavon became one of the first purpose-built multi-furnace ironworks in the world. Today, it is the best preserved 18th century ironworks in Europe.

TRAM WAY ROUND THE BLORENGE

The site the founders' selected for their furnaces was on the side of a hill. A slope was cut back to form a low cliff and three furnaces built against it so that they could be charged with raw materials from the high ground at the rear. At this upper level were also the calcining kilns in which the iron ore was roasted to reduce impurities. Men and boys and even women and girls broke up the ironstone using heavy hammers. Behind the kilns, the open space where coal was burned into coke is now a rugby pitch. Each furnace was a square tapering stone stack enclosing a firebrick-lined vessel. The iron ore, coke and limestone were fed in at the top and the liquid iron and slag tapped off at the bottom. In front were cast houses covering sand pig beds. The steam engine houses which provided the blast were situated across the yard. About 1810, two more furnaces were added plus a second steam engine house.

The iron produced was shipped south to Newport. Thomas Hill constructed a tram road completed in 1817 around the north side of the Blorenge Mountain with a 2400 metre long tunnel at Pwll Du going down on three inclines to the Brecon and Abergavenny Canal at Llanfoist. Wharf. Throughout the day, trains of wooden drams pulled by horses ran on iron wheels along flanged iron rails. Souvenir drawings of these days can be purchased in the area. At Llanfoist, the iron in the drams was unloaded into canal boats for the journey to Newport. And not only iron but coal as well. Coal had been gathered or mined around Blaenavon possibly since Roman times.

ROUTE CAN STILL BE SEEN

The route of the Tramway can still be seen and walked today. From the historic centre of Blaenavon town to the mineral workings on the mountains and along the route of Thomas Hill's inclines down to the leafy canal towpath, the Blaenavon landscape is fascinating to explore. Today, holiday boats can be hired on the Brecon and Abergavenny Canal with its wharves and warehouses not only at Llanfoist but also at Goytre and Govilon.

A major consequence of using the Brecon and Abergavenny Canal was that in 1817 a new forge was set up at Garn-Ddyrys, beside Hill's Tramway. Pig iron could now be taken from the Blaenavon Ironworks to Garn-Ddyrys, forged into wrought iron and shipped out via the Brecon and Abergavenny Canal.

The founder's great grandson sold Blaenavon Ironworks to a joint stock company in 1836. Within two years, as part of a process of modernisation, a water balance tower was

Iron and coal were once unloaded from trams and into canal boats at Llanfoist Wharf.

constructed the remains of which are a rare survivor of its type and a key feature of the site.

The water balance system enabled iron to be lifted to the higher level required for its shipment along Hill's Tramway and casting sand to be sent down. There was a winding wheel at the top suspended in an iron frame. Trams were raised up and let down using giant iron tanks filled with water to provide balance to the load.

A network of tramways spread out from the ironworks to the north and west bringing iron ore, coal and limestone to the furnaces and carting iron away.

In 1854, that new wonder of the age, the railway, courtesy of the Great Western Railway, reached Blaenavon and it became possible to reach the sea at Newport by rail along the bottom of the valley. As a consequence, within six years, Hill's tramway was no longer the preferred export route for iron. Not to be outdone the London North Western Railway extended a tentacle southwards, along the eastern flank of the Coity mountain to reach Blaenavon (High Level) by 1869. A few years later

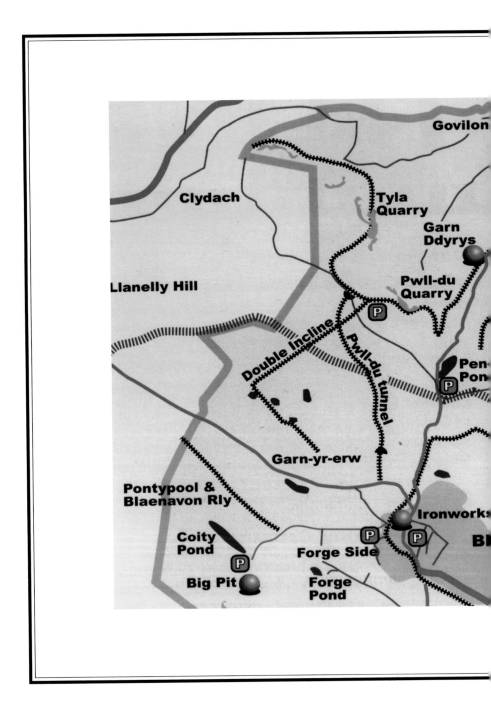

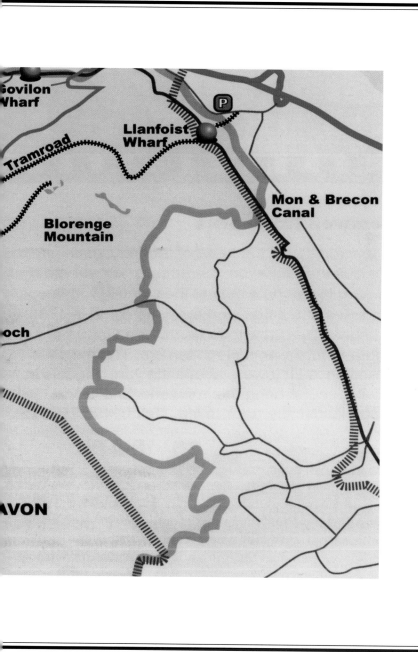

Govilon
Wharf

Llanfoist
Wharf

P

Tramroad

Blorenge
Mountain

Mon & Brecon
Canal

och

AVON

35

Staff welcoming visitors to the Tourist Information Centre at Blaeanavon Ironworks.

the LNWR extended further southward to reach Abersychan and Talywain, where an end on junction was made with yet a further northward thrust by the GWR on a line built by the Monmouthshire Railway and Canal Company. This LNWR/ GWR line later attracted the sobriquet 'Top Line'. Within twenty years there were thus three railway lines out of Blaenavon.

Rail transport provided a new stimulus for investment and development at the ironworks. A new and more modern works was built across the valley at Forgeside and most production switched to the larger and more linear works. Soon iron rails made at Forgeside for the new railways circled the world.

A discovery that was to bring prosperity to Blaenavon

and confirm for all time the role of the town in the history of iron and steel making took place at the original Blaenavon Ironworks in 1878. Steel, a type of modified iron of immense strength, had begun to be made using the new Bessemer converters. But these converter produced useless brittle steel if phosphorous was present.

Sidney Gilchrist Thomas, whose cousin worked at the Ironworks as a chemist, discovered a process allowing the use of iron ore with high phosphoric content to make high quality steel thus enabling unrestricted use of the Bessemer converters and opening up steel making from Russia to America - a major impetus to the Industrial Revolution. In 1878 Andrew Carnegie paid US$250,000 for the rights to use the Gilchrist Thomas process in the United States and a plaque at the old Iron Work's entrance inspired by the American Society of Metallurgists pays tribute to the site as "the birthplace of the basic steel process."

LAST PIT TO CLOSE

The use of readily accessible ore with a higher phosphoric content meant that steel works were best located at the coast, close to supplies of imported ore and as early as 1911 the long-term future of steel making at Blaenavon was in doubt. Final closure came in 1938. At the original ironworks, the last furnace was blown out in 1904 and what remained of the old works used for workshops and briefly as a foundry.

The coming of the railway and surging demand for iron provoked the rapid opening of new collieries in an area already honeycombed with workings. Big Pit was opened in 1860 as the coal winding shaft for nearby Coity Pits and is today a museum which the public can visit and experience conditions 293 feet underground. Big Pit was the last mine in the Blaenavon area to close in 1980 and today is one of the most popular heritage sites in Wales providing a memorable underground experience and with an excellent book and gift shop.

Not only does Blaenavon reflect the technological revolution of the 18th and 19th centuries but also the social

A family almost 300 feet underground at Big Pit

revolution that transformed rural communities into highly populated industrial areas.

In the early days, as word had spread that work was to be had at Blaenavon young men and women trekked in from West Wales, from the West Midlands and from Wiltshire. There was also a steady stream of job seekers from Ireland. By the turn of the 18th century Monmouthshire, in which Blaenavon was then situated, was growing faster than any other county in England and Blaenavon had become the second largest ironworks in Wales after nearby Merthyr Tydfil. Even within a decade of its founding the works employed 350 and was producing 5,400 tons of iron per annum. Rows or houses were run up quickly to provide shelter for the influx of workers.

Homes for key workers built between 1789 and 1792 can still be seen on the site of the old furnaces, architecturally similar to others in the West Midlands from where the founders hailed. Characteristically, the window frames are of iron. The houses at Stack Square were built in pairs with a fireplace and chimney in each end wall and a brick wall separating them. Bedrooms were upstairs with living room and larder below. Cooking would have been done on the living room fire. There was no plumbing or sanitation. At the upper end of Engine Row, close to the road, the taller, three storey building was the company truck shop where workers could obtain goods on credit until they were paid. The pioneer workmen at Blaenavon were far from any shops and the company store satisfied the need yet was the source of much dissatisfaction and unrest. There were many complaints that truck goods were over priced and of poor quality. On payday workers frequently had little money left, if any. The iron workers cottages were occupied until the 1960s. Today they house a permanent exhibiton of models and pictures which bring not only the Ironworks but the entire World Heritage Site to life.

ISOLATED TERRACES STILL EXIST

The Ironworks is maintained by Welsh Historic Monuments (CADW) and the excellent visitor information centre is open to visitors with guided tours by arrangement.

We can easily imagine workmen's houses being dotted around the landscape, close to the furnaces, forges and mines and, indeed, several isloated terraces still exist. But as output increased more than huddles of houses were needed and a town developed at Blaenavon. By 1830 the town had five chapels, five public houses and four shops, many of which can still be seen today. The ornate Workmen's Hall opened in 1895 after £8,000 was collected by local workers at the rate of one halfpenny per week. The building reflects a century of success in iron making and coal mining. Its size can be judged from the fact that today its facilities include a 90-seat cinema, a 380-seat

Blaeanavon Workingman's Hall - a monument to the town's success

auditorium, two licensed bars, and committee rooms. Even to stand in its cavernous rooms is to feel the pride of the working men of the day in themselves, their works and in their country, then, the industrial leader of the world.

Across the street is St. Peter's Church, built by the early ironmasters Thomas Hill and Samuel Hopkins in 1805, with its iron window ledges, structural pillars and even iron grave covers. The church has been paintakingly renovated and is open to the public.

Next door, is St. Peter's School, the oldest works school in Wales, opened in 1816 by Hopkins' sister, Sarah, in memory of her brother. This important building is now being restored as a World Heritage Centre with Heritage Lottery Fund support. The Centre will offer a programme of permanent and rotating exhibitions and even re-enactments. It will have a strong educational and community bias.

Samuel Hopkins' House, the 'Big House', can be seen on Church Road and is now a private nursing home.

NOT ALWAYS SO PEACEFUL

Blaenavon was not always so peaceful. It was here and in the adjacent valleys that industry turned agricultural workers into proletarians, a class swept by all the fashionable beliefs of the 19th and early 20th centuries- in Chartism and trade unionism, in socialism and in rights and fair treatment for the working man, including the all-important right to vote. These quiet streets once echoed to the angry shouts of working class rioters fighting to wrench concessions from their employers or from the government and to the thud of the boots of the soldiers sent to keep them in order. Nearby Merthyr Tydfil, once the greatest iron towns in the world, was the first place in Britain to witness the raising of the Red Flag. The iron, steel and coal industries were characterised by cycles of prosperity and depression. Soon after the General Strike of 1926, 40 percent of the working men were unemployed and hunger and want were widespread.

With the death of iron and steel making at Blaenavon and the closure of its coal mines Blaenavon fell on hard times leaving the somewhat ghostly remains we see today. But 6,000 people still live in the town and local merchants continue to serve the community while looking to increase trade by catering to the growing number of visitors.

Next to the new town library there is an exhibition devoted to Alexander Cordell, a novelist who made industrial South Wales famous with such books as 'Rape Of The fair Country,' 'Hosts Of Rebecca,' 'Song Of The Earth,' 'The Fire People,' and 'This Sweet And Bitter Earth.' "Rape Of The Fair

Country' was set in and around Blaenavon. Leaflets describing a town walk and copies of the novels are available here.

Blaenavon tells us a vital part of the early formative years of the Industrial Revolution as virtually no other site does. It illustrates not only the linear process of technological development but also the integrated nature of the inventions - from coal to coke, to iron, to steel - transported first along pack horse trails, then by horse, next by canal and last by railway. And it provides important insights into the transformation of rustic rural dwellers into the world's first industrial nation.

The Blaenavon World Heritage Site helps us imagine the lives of the workers and their masters as we walk the streets of the town, follow the tramways or ride the rails and canals which once hauled Blaenavon coal, iron and steel from these isolated mountains to markets around the world.

For opening times and admission charges please contact:

Blaenavon Ironworks
Tel: 01495 792615
www.blaenavontic.com

Pontypool & Blaenavon
Railway
Tel: 01495 792263
www.pontypool-
and-blaenavon.co.uk

**Blaenavon Community
Heritage/ Cordell Museum**
Tel: 07930 719110
www.visittorfaen.co.uk

**Big Pit National Mining
Museum of Wales**
Tel: 01495 790311
www.nmgw.ac.uk

Big Pit

Blaenavon,
Torfaen NP4 9XP

Tel: 01495 790311
Fax: 01495
792618
www.nmgw.ac.uk

The simple act of standing in bright, warm sunlight above Big Pit, looking out over the town of Blaenavon and the Blorenge Mountain is a delightful experience for all those who have spent even a few minutes underground experiencing and imagining the traditional life of a South Wales coal miner.

Big Pit was sunk in 1860 and closed in 1980 but it is not for the sake of history that visitors travel from near and far to the National Mining Museum of Wales at Blaenavon.

What attracts people is the prospect of going underground as miners would have gone underground, of walking along tunnels where real men once worked real shifts hewing the black diamonds of South Wales with only a head lamp for light. The dark at the bottom of the shaft was always as much of a surprise as the light up above. Pit ponies kept for long periods in darkness could go crazy when brought to the surface and rebel vigorously when the time came to send them back underground. Some of the stalls of these plucky animals can still be seen, complete with the ponies names.

Blaenavon has a remote feel about it even today and to the Romans who foraged in the outcrops of the Blorenge the journey must have seemed like going to the end of the earth. Blaenavon coal was of high quality and journey to get it they did, perhaps to heat the under floor heating systems in the villas and public buildings of Roman Caerleon, close to modern Newport.

It was a pattern of extraction and transportation that would be repeated until the very last colliery at the head of the valley had closed with the mode of haulage evolving from pack horses and carts, to canals and finally railways.

Coal from the mines of Wales helped drive the steam trains, ships and factory engines which made Britain the Workshop of the World. It also fuelled the blast furnaces from which iron was made, including at the Blaenavon Ironworks, opened in 1789 and now part of the Blaenavon World Heritage Site.

When the visitor stands in daylight above Big Bit today, the entire landscape he sees around him is man-made

reflecting the integration of coal with iron and steel making. Big Pit was by no means the only colliery at Blaenavon. Once iron production commenced the demand for coal rose steadily and the number of collieries increased, littering the landscape with mounds of unsightly waste, today grassed over pleasantly enough.

The need to move the iron and coal from Blaenavon resulted in a network of tramways being created around the Blorenge Mountain to haul the heavy materials for shipment to canals linking the remote site with Newport in the south and Hereford in the north. By the mid-19th century, tramways and canals were rendered obsolete by the new wonder of the age - the railways

Before the opening of Blaenavon Ironworks there was next to nothing at Blaenavon but as output expanded iron workers, coal miners and hauliers were attracted to the area and slowly were built the homes, shops and hotels which have become the town of Blaenavon.

On a fine day, it would have been a pleasant walk to the colliery; in the depth of winter, when it was dark above ground and below and the ground was hard with frost or snow it won't have been very romantic.

Guides at Big Pit have been chosen for their sense of humour and when they turn off all the lights 293 feet underground so that the visitor stands in impenetrable blackness it doesn't do to panic. Miners lived in constant fear of explosions ground, maybe as young as six years old, frightened of the rats that could be heard and felt scurrying about and spending ten to twelve hours a day listening for drams of coal. When the drams arrived, pushed and pulled either by human muscle or pit ponies, their job was to open and close airdoors in front and behind.

Sometimes they were hungry. Often they were tired and fell asleep. Sometimes the older boys and girls would haul the heavy drams weighing about sixty eight kilogrammes like beasts of burden, a chain girdle around their middles and between their legs. Most young girls were lucky enough to be

able to work at the pit top emptying or tipping trams. The work made children tough and resilient or they risked serious injury.

When the miner himself wanted to stop for a bite to eat there was no place to squat down other than on the coal he had been working all shift and should the need arise to relieve himself there was no place other than the coal where he had just eaten. He worked in a stall which was narrow with a low roof and always wet. He had to crouch and scramble over rocks and stones before he could begin his work and his pay depended on how much was dug.

For boys and girls or men and boys, after the shift there was a long walk home, dirty, wet and exhausted. Then a wash in a tin bath and hot meal before sleep in a crowded room where most of the family might be resting.

These details of the lives of miners are mostly described to the visitor by guides who are themselves ex-miners. Their inimitable Welsh good humour makes the visit underground not only informative but enjoyable. The men, like the pit itself, form an unforgettable experience. Perhaps that is why over 120,000 people now visit Big Pit every year, 30 percent of them from overseas, majority from France and Germany but with ten other European countries represented and many more from further afield.

Big Pit is still classed as a working colliery and must comply with the Mines and Quarries Act safety legislation. Fifty staff look after the mine's thousands of visitors. During twenty years as a museum, Big Pit has attracted over two million visitors.

Back on the surface after a memorable adventure underground, there is a cafeteria for hot or cold drinks and snacks. There is also a shop selling coal mining memorabilia, publications and gifts, including tapes of the world famous Welsh male voice choirs.

Photo courtesy of Bernard Morton

The route of the Pontypool and Blaenavon Railway taken by tourists makes it the steepest standard gauge preserved passenger carrying line in Britain. The steep pull up the line ensures some spectacular starts for the locomotives. At 1,300 feet, the northern halt is the highest and probably the most windswept station in England and Wales. The Whistle Inn, next to the halt is famous for its collection of miners' lamps. A ride on the railway is a trip through a landscape which still contains a fascinating mix of relics from the days of steel and coal.

The Wenallt

Gilwern,
Nr. Abergavenny,
Gwent
NP7 OHP.
Tel: 01873 830694

Charming and cozy 16th century Welsh longhouse with all mod cons at the foot of the Blorenge Mountain in the Brecon Beacons National Park. Minutes from Blaenavon town, Big Pit, the Brecon Mountain Railway and the Monmouthshire & Brecon Canal. Ideal also for walking, pony trekking, sailing or just looking around the beautiful countryside and the old market towns. From M4 junction 24 to Abergavenny via A449 and then via A465.

Mill Farm

Cwmavon, Nr, Pontypool, Torfaen NP4 8XJ. Fax/phone: 01495 774588

Relax in the comfort of this 15th century farmhouse, with its 'Olde Worlde' features, antique furniture and heated swimming pool in lounge. Welsh breakfast is served until noon. Gardens, terraces and 1,000-year-old woodlands. Situated five minutes from Blaenavon World Heritage Site and an ideal base for exploring other historic sites and attractions in South Wales.

Cordell Country Inn

Blaenavon Road,
Govilon,
Abergavenny,
Monmouthshire,
NP7 9NY.
Tel: 01873 830436.
Fax: 01495 310564
Email: andweed@aol.com

In Brecon Beacons National Park, this is absolutely the closest accommodation to Blaenavon. Ideal for walks along the route of the old tramways, once used to haul iron and coal. Long association with the books of industrial revolution novelist, Alexander Cordell, and with heritage publisher, Chris Barber. Spectacular views from en suite rooms. Friendly hosts and substantial Welsh breakfast.

Hardwick Farm

Hardwick,
Abergavenny,
Monmouthshire
NP7 9BT
Tel: 01873 853513
Fax: 01873 854238
Email:
carol.hardwickfarm@virgin.net
Website: www.downourlane.co.uk/8.htm

A working 230 acre dairy and arable farm set in the picturesque Usk Valley on the edge of the Brecon Beacons National Park. Over the Blorenge Mountain from Blaenavon World Heritage Site and close to the Brecon & Monmouthshire Canal M4 junction 24 towards Monmouth, A449 take 2nd exit signposted Abergavenny A40. From Abergavenny take A4042 and Hardwick Farm is 1/2 mile on the right.

Ty-Cooke Farm

Mamhilad, Pontypool. Monmouthshire NP4 8QZ.
Tel/fax:
Tel: 01873 880382.
Email: tycookefarm@hotmail.com

Traditionally furnished 18th century farmhouse on family run beef and sheep farm, 3/4 mile from Goytre Wharf on the beautiful Monmouthshire-Brecon Canal. Deep in rural Monmouthsire but only minutes from the Blaenavon World Heritage Site. Junction 25A off the M4 towards Abergavenny and from Abergavenny via the A4042 to Pontypool. Pub serving excellent meals within 10 minute walk.

Yew Tree Farm

Llanellen, Nr. Abergavenny, Gwent NP7 9LB
Tel: 01873 854307
email: groseandcollanellen@ukonline.co.uk
Website: www.communities.msn.co.uk/YewTreeFarmBedBreakfastAccommodation

A working 40-acre smallholding in the Brecon Beacons National Park, ideal for exploring the Blaenavon World Heritage Site, and an area rich in history, border castles, Roman antiquities and rural life. The Monmouthshire & Brecon Canal intersects the approach road via a charming rustic track and it is possible to walk through the breathtaking countryside to Blaenavon.

Abergavenny Hotel

21, Monmouth Road, Abergavenny NP7 5HF
Tel:01873 855324

In the heart of the old market town of Abergavenny, adjacent to Tourist Information Centre and car park and close to all bus and rail services. A super convenient, recently refurbished pub with en suite rooms, convivial pub atmosphere and delectable dining.

Junction Cottage

Canal Basin, Pontymoile, Pontypool NP4 8ER

Tel: 0800 542 2663. Fax: 01495 755877
Email: junctioncottage@messages.co.uk
Website: www.junctioncottage.co.uk
Self-catering historic canal toll house on the Monmouthshire-Brecon Canal. Perfect ambiance for visit to Blaenavon World Heritage Site. The canal was once a main artery for the shipment of iron and coal from South Wales to the world. Junction Cottage is ideal for heritage tourism as well as for a relaxing time walking, cycling or just watching the boats go by.

Highfield House

6, Belmont Road,
Abergavenny,
Monmouthshire
NP7 5HN.
Tel: 01873 852371
Fax: 01873 858180

bookings@highfieldabergavenny.co.uk
www.highfieldabergavenny.co.uk

Highfield House is a comfortable Victorian villa in the heart of the market town of Abergavenny. It offers a warm, friendly base from which you can explore the Blaenavon World Heritage Site or discover the delights of the Welsh borders with its quaint and rustic towns and villages, historic castles and superb rivers and mountains.

Pentre Court

Llanwenarth Citra,
Abergavenny,
Monmouthshire
NP7 7EW
Tel: 01873 853545.
email: judith@pentrecourt.com.
www.pentrecourt.com

Pentre Court is a small Georgian Grade II listed country house just outside Abergavenny on the A40 to Brecon. The house recaptures the feel of the past but with modern conveniences and is set in 4 acres of wooded gardens on the banks of the Nantiago. There are fine views from the terrace across the Usk Valley to the Blorenge Mountain. 2 WTB bed and breakfast stars and Welcome International Host certificate. Accredited member of Taste of Wales.

Rhiw Ffranc Farm

Pentwyn,
Abersychan,
Nr. Pontypool,
Torfaen NP4 7TJ.
Fax/phone:
01495 775069

Email: rhiwffrancfarm@aol.com
WTB 4 Star. Website: www.
rhiwffrancfarmholidayapartments.co.uk

Three self-catering apartments to accommodate 1-14 guests in converted early 19th century iron workers' cottages just 4 miles from Blaenavon World Heritage Site. Rich in its own industrial heritage and set peacefully in 90 acres, Rhiw Ffranc Farm is now a nature lover's paradise participating in "Tir Gofal" (land in care) and the Agri-environmental Scheme. Open all year with owner on site to welcome you.

Hopyard Farm Cottages

Govilon,
Abergavenny,
Monmouthshire,
NP7 9SE
Fax/phone:
01873 830219

Email: diana@hopyardcottages.co.uk

Located only four miles from the Blaenavon World Heritage Site and just off the Cordell Country Route, Hopyard Farm Cottages provide the ideal base to explore this fascinating area. This former dairy farm offers four self-catering, fully modernized cottages. Facilities on the farm include a children's play area, laundry room, boules court, ample car parking and a comprehensive range of cycles for hire.

Canal Mania
In The Industrial
Revolution

As domestic and overseas trade grew throughout the 18th century transport was a persistent bottleneck.

There have been many attempts to explain the veritable fever of enterprise and speculation which gripped Britain with gathering momentum as the 18th century unfolded.

Whatever the cause, more and more raw materials were being transported and more and more finished goods were shipped to markets further and further afield.

But how to do this? In the early part of the 18th century the only roads were narrow lanes and paths barely suitable for the lines of pack animals which were used to carry goods. Quantities were relatively small, costs high and breakages of fragile items legion. In wet weather, the roads became impassable.

At first, the answer was seen to lie in the improvement of the rustic road system and between 1750 and 1770 there was a road mania in which the number of turnpike roads increased by five hundred percent. More people travelled to more places in less time. A major benefit was that instead of pack animals, increasing quantities of goods were hauled by wagons but costs remained high. The world famous iron bridge completed in 1779 by the Coalbrookdale Company across the River Severn, then a busy waterway for shipping, was part of this fever.

By the 1780s iron was being put to more uses than ever before and the demand for the coke with which it was smelted had led to a growing demand for coal. At the same time, steam, which also relied on coal, was becoming ever more popular as its incredible potential as a source of motive power became daily more obvious.

Nothing was more important to the improvement in Britain's transport system than finding a way of diminishing the cost of transporting coal. The way found was canals.

Britain's first canal was dug by the Duke of Bridgewater between 1759 and 1761 to carry coal from his estates at Worsley to the burgeoning city of Manchester where it was said to have halved the price. The Duke was lucky to have found the services of James Brindley, an unschooled millwright, because his proposed canal had to be cut via underground mine workings and would require an aqueduct over the River Irwell. Brindley solved the engineering challenges and made his reputation in the process.

A few of the more major navigable rivers had already been deepened and even canalized for this purpose and all coal from Newcastle reached London and the south of England not by road but by sea.

Not only could water transport halve the price of coal at its destination but as Josiah Wedgwood found at his Etruria Works, a single barge could carry the equivalent of a hundred pack horses. So, whether the goods to be transported were bulky and heavy like coal or pig iron or small and perhaps fragile like Wedgwood's pottery or Matthew Boulton's Birmingham "toys," canal transport had the edge over anything else available.

Brindley's engineering feats soon became in so much demand that he literally worked himself to death. Backed by the Duke of Bridgewater, he engineered the Manchester to Liverpool Canal in 1767 and in 1777 his Grand Trunk Canal, linking the Mersey with the Trent via the Staffordshire Potteries was completed. Canals became so important that Adam Smith was brought to declare that Britain's very industrial expansion depended upon them.

Eventually canal building would come to involve veritable armies of navvies toiling to link remote communities and bring markets ever closer to suppliers. The engineering obstacles were sometimes formidable and, like Brindley, another engineer who solved them in bold style was Thomas Telford.

Telford's aqueduct on the Ellesmere Canal at Pontcysyllte near Llangollen - one of the "Wonders of Wales" - is even today an awesomely breathtaking site 127 feet above the River Dee and even more breathtaking to pass over in a narrow boat with seemingly little separating the vessel from the infinity of empty sky. At nearby Chirk another beautifully graceful Telford aqueduct is rivalled by an inevitably taller railway viaduct completed between 1846 and 1848. Water from the Darkie Tunnel spills out at the feet of these massive stone and brick arches, providing a visual "feast" for the canal enthusiast.

COMPLEX NETWORK

By the beginning of the 19th century, Britain's manufacturing districts were linked to major markets and ports by a complex network of interlinked canals - many of which survive.

Today, the canals are no longer the scene of bargees jostling for position at crowded locks or of passengers disembarking at inland basins to spend a convivial night in a travellers' hotel.

But they remain surprisingly crowded, albeit with voyagers and holiday makers who prefer the unhurried pace of water transport and the enjoyment of some of Britain's most beautiful rural scenery. British Waterways manages around two thirds of the extant 3,000 miles of canals and inland waterways in Britain, hosting 25,000 licensed boats.

For those interested in industrial heritage, the waterways are rich in nostalgia passing through and over many a lock, basin, tunnel and bridge which in their day were wonders of the time and ending up in the centre of towns and cities brought dramatically to life by the Industrial Revolution, towns such as Manchester, Birmingham, Sheffield and Leeds. Along the way, in or out of urban areas, the modern canal user will have no problem finding a "watering hole" and, at some wharves, restaurants, shopping and even entertainment. He or she may even be lucky enough to find a festival in full swing.

After decades of decline, the cultural and economic importance of Britain's canals and rivers is at last being realized. Throughout its 2,000-mile (3,219 kilometres) network, British Waterways cares for almost 3,000 listed buildings and over 130 scheduled ancient monuments, together representing one of the United Kingdom's best collections of industrial heritage. Structures ranging from humble warehouses and cottages, to grandiose bridges and soaring aqueducts make up a 200-year old network which still works to its original purpose. There are 1,520 locks, 3,270 bridges, 60 tunnels, 450 aqueducts, 1,036 lock cottages and dwellings and 89 reservoirs in the system. Unexpectedly, the modern network also includes 1,000 wildlife conservation areas, 100 sites of Special Scientific Interest and 600 miles of hedgerow.

WORKING HERITAGE

The fact that inland waterways are a 'working heritage' sets them apart from other historic structures and demands a unique approach to their management and conservation. British Waterways aims to achieve a balance in protecting the historic integrity of the waterways whilst allowing them to flourish. The most successful waterside regeneration schemes combine the old with the new - retaining or refurbishing historic canal buildings and using good, complementary modern design.

The number of visitors to the canals are testimony to the success of this approach. Around 10 million visitors each year make 160 million visits. Remarkably, freight is actually returning to the canals and with the government's policy of transferring 3.5 percent of road freight to inland waterways and coastal routes volumes can only be expected to increase.

British Waterways

Pontcysyllte Aqueduct

The highest and biggest in the British isles, the towering aqueduct at Pontcysyllte is one of the most dramatic features on the national 2,000-mile waterway network.

Built by renowned engineers Thomas Telford and William Jessop, the aqueduct is a Scheduled Ancient Monument, a candidate for World Heritage status and a Grade 1 listed structure widely known as 'one of the wonders of Wales.'

Completed in 1805 by the Ellesmere Canal Company, the aqueduct carries the Llangollen Canal across the River Dee, turning it into a waterway in the sky - over 120 feet (39 metres) high and over 1,000 feet (305 metres) long.

One of the most innovative features of the aqueduct is Telford's decision to lay an iron, water-carrying trough on top of a row of stone piers. Dovetail joints in the iron trough were sealed with a highly successful combination of Welsh flannel and lead dipped in liquid sugar. The craftsmanship of the stonework is equally impressive, with very thin masonry joints bonded by a mortar made from a mixture of ox-blood and lime.

The aqueduct successfully linked Llangollen with the rest of the Shropshire Union Canal system - and continues to work today. The aqueduct originally carried coal from local mines, but it also supplied water, taken from the Dee at Horseshoe Falls (also built by Telford) and fed into the rest of the Shropshire Union Canal. Today the structure continues to carry over 50 million litres of water every day to supply the water needs of southern Cheshire.

The aqueduct remains virtually unchanged since it was opened, apart from refurbishment to the balustrade and towpath, and more than 10,000 boats and 25,000 pedestrians cross it each year.

The Falkirk Wheel

Far from dying out in the face of competition from railways and road transport, Britain's waterways have taken on a new lease of life with the explosion in the number of recreational users.

But the Falkirk Wheel, the only one of its kind in the world, is not just putting something old to a new use. It's something completely new and utterly different. The promotional brochures say that it defies belief.

British Waterways Scotland cares for and conserves more than 200 miles of waterways and the Millennium Link project has revived the Forth and Clyde coast-to-coast ship canal and the Union Canal, relinking Edinburgh and Glasgow by waterway for the first time in many years.

Replacing a flight of 19th century locks which closed in the 1930s, the Falkirk Wheel is the world's first rotating

boat lift and the first boat lift to be built in Britain since the Anderton Boat lift in Cheshire was completed in 1875.

In addition to the Wheel, the canal interchange project includes a visitor centre, new section of canal, two aqueducts, three locks, a tunnel, a railway bridge and a canal basin.

The only structure of its kind in the world, at 115 feet (35 metres) the Wheel is the height of eight double-decker buses. It is 115 feet (35 metres) wide and 100 feet (30 metres) long.

The Wheel can lift loads of 600 tonnes, the approximate weight of 100 adult African elephants. It carries eight or more boats at a time and a single trip takes 15 minutes.

The adventure begins at the Visitor Centre and Boardwalk where you can idle awhile to watch the incredible sight of entire boats rotating skywards or board one yourself for the journey upwards to cross an aqueduct high above the ground and thrill to a tunnel lights show. Even for those who never venture onto it the Falkirk Wheel is brought to life within the Visitor centre by means of plasma screens, tracker balls and a host of interactive exhibits.

Over a quarter-of-a-million people a-year visit the Falkirk Wheel making it one of the most visited attractions in the British Isles.

For information call: 08700 500 208 or see www.thefalkirkwheel.co.uk

The Anderton Boat Lift

The Anderton Boat Lift at Northwich, Cheshire, has been described as one of the wonders of the Industrial Revolution and one of the greatest monuments to Britain's canal era.

First opened in 1875 and re-adapted to a cogs and pulley system in 1908, Anderton is internationally significant and a prototype for similar boat lifts in Belgium, France and Canada. Linking the River Weaver to the Trent and Mersey Canal 50 feet above, the lift closed in 1983 due to corrosion discovered during a routine maintenance inspection.

Those who take the Trip Boat on the 50 foot upward voyage need have no worries about safety. More than £7 million has been spent restoring this magnificent example of Victorian engineering involving 3,000 components being dismantled, cleaned, repaired and reassembled like a giant Mecanno set.

The operation of the lift is deceptively simple. Two counter balanced tanks, supported on massive hydraulic rams and sealed by watertight doors, carried boats between the two navigations. Assisted by a steam accumulator, a small quantity of water was drawn from the lower tank to create a difference in weight large enough to cause the heavier tank to sink and the other to rise.

The Trip Boat used by visitors is also vintage. It was converted from a former maintenance craft which once worked on the Leeds and Liverpool Canal.

The excitement of the ride may be enough for some but for people with a thirst to find out more there is an exhibition centre which using displays and videos tells the full story of the Anderton Boat Lift and its restoration.

The Operations Centre is also open to visitors and provides an opportunity to watch the lift at work and even to ask searching questions of its operators. Interactive exhibits allow visitors the chance of experiencing the challenge of the Lift for themselves. The Centre contains a gift shop and cafe.

For information call: 01606 786777 or see www.andertonboatlift.co.uk

Standedge Tunnel

Two hundred years ago, fifty men gave their lives digging the longest canal tunnel in Britain - three-and-a-half miles long, deep beneath the Pennines. At 645 feet above sea level it was the highest in the country and at 638 feet below the surface it holds the record for being the deepest tunnel in the British Isles.

Sealed for half a century and dubbed the 'impossible restoration,' Standedge Tunnel is now delighting and thrilling modern visitors.

The Tunnel, also known as one of the Severn Wonders of the Waterways, was cut in the 18th century by navvies using candlelight and in appalling conditions. The Tunnel was a crucial component in the dramatic 20-mile long Huddersfield Narrow Canal and was completed in 1811 under the supervision of the famous canal engineer, Thomas Telford.

Visitors to the Tunnel begin their adventure at the Standedge Visitor Centre set up inside a refurbished trans-shipment centre which straddles the Canal.

Inside the Centre, visitors board custom built electric boats in which guides help bring the story of the Standedge Tunnel vividly to life. There are also two floors of interactive activities which make a visit to the Tunnel exciting and informative for the whole family.

Boats and even hikers can now pass safely through the Tunnel, hewn with such difficulty and now expertly restored to provide fascination and fun to the modern visitor.

For information call:
01484 844298 or see
www.standedge.co.uk

The Boat Museum, Ellesmere Port

The cut which marked the opening of the canal age in Britain is usually said to have been the navigation built in 1761 by the Duke of Bridgewater to link his mines at Worsley with the rapidly growing city of Manchester where, as the Industrial Revolution unfolded, the demand for coal grew exponentially.

The coal was brought out of the Duke's mines via underground canals and an example of the long and narrow craft used in the tunnels can still be seen at the Boat Museum at Ellesmere Port in Cheshire.

The boats were known as Starvationers because their ribs were exposed and they were legged or pulled from rings in the roof, often by women and children. The Starvationer in the Boat Museum is the oldest canal boat in its collection.

In fact, the very first canal was the Sankey Brook Navigation cut from the Mersey to St. Helens in 1757 to facilitate the trade in salt and coal between Cheshire and Lancashire.

Ellesmere Port, close to the Mersey, was destined to become a major junction on the canal system linking Liverpool and its great waterway with industrial towns on the rivers Severn, Dee and Trent and eventually locking in to 3,000 miles of navigations nationwide including the Shropshire Union Canal, the Manchester Ship Canal, the Trent and Mersey Canal and the Birmingham and Liverpool Junction Canal.

With increased traffic in the early part of the 19th century the docks and the town of Ellesmere grew rapidly. It became located at the centre of a spider's web of watery arteries ferrying people and goods around Britain at a time when there were no proper roads and, until the 1830s and 40s, few railways.

Locks and pumping stations were needed to enable canal boats to pass from one part of the system to another; stables were built to house the horses which pulled the barges from towpaths running along the sides of the canals. Workshops were installed for the repair and even the building of boats and to manufacture the materials needed for lock gate construction.

Docks were required so that the narrow boats could berth. Warehouses multiplied for the storage of coal, flour, iron, clay, china products and the myriad outpourings of Britain's burgeoning factories. Three flour mills were erected on the site. With the coming of the railway age, connections were built so that railway wagons could load and discharge from boats below.

And of course there were homes for senior employees and offices.

Inside the Boat Museum there are aerial views which show in detail what the Ellesmere Port complex looked like during its hey day. With the aid of maps and a detailed guide book visitors will be fascinated to be able to tour surviving parts of this formidable complex, in many ways structurally and architecturally very specific to the canals.

The Island Warehouse is home to an exhibition which tells the story of the canals, the boats and of the people who worked them, men and women, indeed, whole families, who often spent their entire working lives in the narrow boats.

The Pump House contains four steam-driven pumping engines once used to power the hydraulic cranes and capstans around the dock complex and the Blacksmith's Forge has been renovated to its original form when it was used for the manufacture and repair of chain.

The highlight of a visit to the Boat Museum has to be its floating collection. Fortunately, many of the boats can be boarded and a way of life long gone can be vividly recalled as a result. You can even take a short trip.

The collection ranges from small coracles through pleasure, maintenance and narrow boats to barges and larger craft, including tugs. Canals had to be kept open throughout the year so there is even an example of an ice breaker. Weeds had to be cleared so there is a weed cutter. And the canals could not be allowed to silt up so there is a steam-powered dredger.

Boats are generally made of wood, iron and steel

or a mixture of both and the Boat Museum has examples of all the
major types as well as displays illustrating construction
techniques. Canal buffs will be ecstatic with the large number of
publications about canals together with other canal memorabilia
on sale in the gift shop.

**For information call: 0151 355 5017 or see
www.boatmuseum.org.uk**

National Waterways Museum, Gloucester

There is so much information about canals at the National Waterways Museum at Gloucester that it is easy to imagine that all we have to do is step outside to find the age of canals still with us.

It is an impression enhanced by the fact that the imposing multi-storey Victorian building which houses the museum, Llanthony Warehouse, was the last of the great corn stores to be opened at Gloucester Docks in 1873 during a time when Gloucester became a centre for the corn trade after foreign grain was first allowed into Britain in the 1840s. In the hey-day of the corn trade there were 15 major corn warehouses, two dock basins and a complex network of rail lines covering some 22 acres. By the 1920s, other ports had taken much of the trade and Gloucester's great warehouses were often used for other purposes ranging from the storage of general cargo to show-rooms.

Llanthony Warehouse is located right on the dock enabling visitors to plunge into the ever fascinating world of canals even before they enter the museum. Not only can they enter a number of craft but it is even possible to go for a trip and even to hire one privately.

Moored at the quayside is the Sabrina 5, built to carry dry cargo in crates. The Northwich is an unpowered narrow boat made of iron and wood which was towed by horse or a motor boat. The Oak was one of the first narrowboats to be welded rather than rivetted. The No 4 Steam Dredger was built in Holland and used to keep the docks at Gloucester and Sharpness free from silt. The Bantam Tug Walsall is a major exhibit inside the museum in the boat gallery on Level 1. The little tugs were used to push barges along the canals.

Level 1 of the museum shows how the narrow boats were moved along the canals, at first by gangs of men and then by horses or donkeys. Later, steam was used but there were

difficulties. The steam engine was often too large for the boat. Using it sometimes meant that so much space was occupied that an unpowered trailer had to be towed counting much of the cargo displaced by the engine. In fact, horses were still used until the 1950s. Around the beginning of the 20th century 'crude oil' engines were first fitted to canal boats.

Thousands of boats were constructed and maintained in the hundreds of boatyards or docks found on Britain's canals and rivers and Level 1 reveals the conditions in which the wooden, composite, iron and steel craft were not only built but maintained. For repairs, the narrowboats were winched sideways up a slipway and a large steam engine in the boat gallery illustrates the kind of power required.

Llanthony Yard has been created at the museum as an example of a canal repair yard and includes a blacksmith's forge, carpenter's workshop, stable and tackroom, engine room and a general workshop where museum conservation and maintenance work is carried out.

Because Llanthony Warehouse is a multi-storey building the museum's collections are on several levels.

Level 2 houses displays which take up the story of the canals in 1793 - the very height of canal mania - the year when more proposals for the building of canals were put before Parliament than ever before. Vivid and lifelike displays show the kind of people who invested in the canals, the navvies who dug them and the people who operated and used them. Surprisingly, we learn that the canal boats were used to carry passengers as well as freight and that some tunnels were so low and narrow that a popular way of getting boats through was for a person to lie down sideways on the top of the boat and push it along with his (or her) legs. This was known as "legging." On this level visitors can see a host of photographs of the canal boats at work seemingly carrying every kind of cargo from coal and china clay to milk and chocolate.

Building the hundreds of miles of waterways sometimes requiring bridges, tunnels and aqueducts and often involving locks and pumping stations was a major engineering feat and Level 3 of the National Waterways Museum is devoted to displays providing revealing insights into who built Britain's canals and how they did it. Of course, after they were built, it is easy to forget that canals need maintenance and the site of diving suits among the displays reminds us that there was an element of life on the canals that had to go on underwater as well as on the surface.

Modern visitors are as fascinated by the lives of the boat people as they are by the boats themselves and Level 3 includes many graphic illustrations of what life afloat was like for the boatmen and their families. There are instructive contrasts between the romance and the reality of life in the narrowboats with the reality including unbelievably cramped conditions in which the boatman, his wife and many children might spend a significant portion of their lives. Earning a living on the canals was hard work. Days began early and ended late. Children seldom had time for schooling and they often helped by leading the horse, setting the locks or steering the boat.

Visiting the National Waterways Museum is by no mans only a matter of looking and learning. The visitor is drawn directly into the world of the canals and narrow boats by interactive elements such as the Waterways Age Share Dealing Game and by touch-screens that allow the design and painting of a narrow boat. You can find out what it was like to be a dock worker as you hoist cargo sacks and for children there is a marvellous interactive gallery and family room for 'kids of all ages.' Here, weights and pulleys, water play areas, period costume, giant jigsaw puzzles and brass rubbings bring history to life.

For information call: 01452 318054 or see www.nwm.org.uk

Gloucester Docks

Gloucester Docks sit at the junction of the River Severn and the Sharpness & Gloucester Canal begun in 1794 and completed in 1827. The area comprises an important collection of historic and listed structures with warehouses, dry docks boat yards and even a rare mariners' chapel. Many of the evocative buildings have been regenerated and converted to new uses and the docks today includes two museums, a marina, retail outlets, restaurants and offices with ambitious plans for still more retail, office and housing development in the future.

The Canal Museum, Stoke Bruerne

Stoke Bruerne Canal Museum on the Grand Union Canal near Northampton takes an affectionate look back to the heyday of the canal era. The canal was begun in 1793 and after almost insuperable difficulties, completed in 1800, except for the Blisworth Tunnel, which opened five years later.

Housed in a restored corn mill in the picturesque village of Stoke Bruerne, with its humped-backed bridge, canal side inn and rustic lock, the museum vividly tells the story of Britain's inland waterways, especially the men and women who worked on them.

We meet the "Father of Inland Navigation', Francis Egerton, the 3rd Duke of Bridgewater and the brilliant engineers who, with no example to guide them, succeeded in a short time in creating a revolutionary nationwide transport system - James Brindley, Thomas Telford, John Rennie and William Jessop. Many of their constructions remain is use today and some, like the Pontcysyllte Aqueduct are breathtaking in their audacity. Telford's own large-scale model of one of the spans of the aqueduct can be seen at the museum. The early canals were built very largely by private enterprise and plans and subscription lists dating from the 18th century are on display. There is also a collection of the badges, coins and tokens issued by the old canal companies.

The culture of the men and women who crewed the narrow boats became very distinctive, almost making them a race apart. Up and down the narrow canals the boat-folk formed a closely-knit community, much intermarried, with a rigid ceremonial for the weddings, christenings and other big occasions that brought them together from time to time. Canalside pubs - like to Boat Inn opposite the museum - were their dance halls,with beer and melodeon to set their feet moving.

There was a tradition for everything, from the placing

of their painted water cans to their intricate rope work. There was even a rigid protocol in the matter of dress. The livery of Morton & Clayton's steam-driven narrow boats included corduroy trousers, brass buttoned waistcoat with velvet collar and braided braces.

One of the first things to catch the eye of a visitor to the museum is a full-size, true colour model of a narrow boat cabin, decorated and furnished as it would have been by the proudest boatmen of the old school. Brass ornaments gleam shiny-bright among floral patterned curtains and 'lace' plates. There, too, is the boatman's melodeon. At night a seat on one side of the narrow boat became a single bed while across the back a double bed folded down; curtains between would be discreetly drawn.

The boats were mostly decorated using what has become known as the 'roses and castles' design - not only the boats but all domestic utensils. Replicas of these are widely available to buyers at museums and retail outlets throughout the canal system. Visitors to the museum can compare boat-folk possessions from all parts of the country and try to spot the subtle design differences which existed from one canal system to another.

Stoke Bruerne is home to a large and fascinating collection of boat paraphernalia ranging from the rope work used on boat fenders to the ear protectors used to keep flies away from the ears of the horses pulling the boats along the towpaths. As steam and then diesel power developed the use of horses declines and the museum's displays show how the changes were gradually accommodated. Moving the boats was not only a matter of horsepower and engine power. Before steam tugs arrived, there was only one way of getting a boat through a tunnel which had no towing path and that was manpower. While the horse was walked over the top of the hill the boatman and his crew 'shafted' or 'legged' through or pulled on chains fixed to the walls of the tunnel. In some tunnels, and Blisworth Tunnel near the museum is one, registered 'leggers' were employed, men whose sole job was to perform this uncongenial service.

Locks, boat lifts and inclined planes were all used to move boats from one level to another. Inclined planes were sloping railways up and down which boats were drawn by one method or another. The museum has a giant model of the Anderton Boat Lift, in real life, now restored and popular with visitors as well as models and diagrams illustrating how the narrow boats were moved around and even how the boats were weighed to make toll charging easy.

Stoke Bruerne is a very different but complementary experience to viewing the collections at the two other museums operated by The Waterways trust at Ellesmere and Gloucester. Prints, photographs, maps, documents, boat relics, brasses, decorative crochet and lace work, traditional boat-folk possessions, models, boat people's suits, dresses, skirts and bonnets have been assembled from all parts of British Waterways to make the past come vividly to life.

For information call: 01604 862229 or see www.thewaterwaystrust.co.uk

Crofton
Pumping Station

C rofton Pumping Station is a surprising
fragment of industry in an otherwise
idyllic rural setting. When it was first built
in the early 19th century, the townsmen who manned it felt as if
they were being posted to the back of beyond. Today, far from
deterring, its lonely location beside the Kennet and Avon Canal,
commends it to modern urbanites hungry for the tranquillity of
rural life.

But ironically it is not only the sights and sounds of country life that draw visitors to Crofton from April to September so much as the enthralling sight of an engine as big as a building in full steam.

Just as today it is difficult to imagine a computer the size of a room, so, too, it boggles the imagination to see and feel the primitive power of an engine so huge that it stands three storeys tall.

At Crofton Pumping Station, near Marlborough, visitors see not only one of these steam Goliaths but two.

It is no accident that the earliest steam engines were developed for the purpose of pumping.

In the 17th century the tin miners of Cornwall longed for a way of keeping water out of their ever-deepening shafts. In 1698, Thomas Savery used steam to power a simple pump consisting of a boiler and a condenser fitted with pipes, one of which went down into the mine and the other to the surface.

NEWCOMEN'S BREAKTHROUGH

But the real breakthrough in the use of steam came in 1708 when Thomas Newcomen invented an engine consisting of a huge timber beam which could be made to rock to and fro high above the ground. At one end was a piston and at the other a pump.

Newcomen's engine was put to use not in the tin mines but in the collieries opening up around Britain as coal replaced timber as Britain's primary fuel. Coal output doubled between 1700 and 1750 and by 1800 stood at ten million tons.

It was often to transport coal that canals were developed from the mid-18th century onwards but with roads often impassable and the capacity of pack animals and waggons severely limited, canal transport was attractive to anyone wishing to ship heavy, bulky and even fragile goods.

In the 18th century the city of Bristol was a major emporium and gateway to Britain's trading and imperial interests

The beam gallery

in Africa and the Americas. The 87-miles long Kennet and Avon Canal was from the outset one of the most important in Britain, linking Bristol with London. Without the canal, goods and passengers not only from the Americas but even the Far East, disembarked at West Country ports, faced a slow journey to the capital by horse, carriage or waggon. The journey by sea could be even slower and fraught with contrary winds and savage storms which saw many a vessel run aground on rocky south coast shores.

The River Kennet was canalized in 1723, the Avon in 1727 and the 57 miles of man-made waterway linking Newbury to Bath were constructed between 1794 and 1810.

The summit of the Canal lies between Crofton and Burbage and is 450 feet above sea level and 40 feet higher than any reliable local water sources. It was a problem that cried out for a pump and a flight of locks as a solution.

In 1794, the canal engineer William Jessop put forward a scheme involving 12 locks and a steam engine to raise the water. Ten locks were eventually built and the pumping station established at Crofton.

By this time the work of Savery and Newcomen had long been overtaken by the discoveries and inventions of James Watt. In partnership with Matthew Boulton of Birmingham, Watt's steam engines soon came to dominate motive power, revolutionizing whole industries. The first Boulton and Watt steam engine went into service at Crofton in 1809 and a second in 1812.

It is the 1812 steam engine that visitors to Crofton see today, the oldest steam powered beam engine in the world, still in its original building and doing its original job of pumping water to the highest point on the Kennet and Avon Canal.

The Canal is often described as 'Britain's best loved canal" containing many architectural marvels such as the Crofton Pumping Station and the Avoncliff and Dundas Aqueducts, near Bradford-on-Avon and Bath respectively. The waterway crosses some of the most beautiful landscapes in England, passing through downland, woods and farmland with abundant wild life at every point.

Like the canal itself, Crofton Pumping Station has been restored and is maintained by a team of enthusiastic volunteers. A little booklet in its cafe-cum-gift shop captures the excitement of the restoration adventure which began in 1968, an adventure which showed both the determination and the love of the Station's volunteers for the job that had to be done.

English Heritage, central and local government and private individuals donated the money, extensive surveys were carried out by volunteer experts, prisoners from Aylesbury goal helped dig out sections of the flues linking the steam boilers to the 46 foot chimney, (in 1997 restored to its original 82 feet) members of the Bristol Aeroplane Company Sub-Aqua Club and the Marlborough Sub-Aqua Club dived under water to inspect the foot of the well and the brickwork in the culvert. Boys from the Worting St. Thomas Scout Troop scoured and repainted the outside of the boiler and then descaled the exterior. It was an incredible mobilization to save a heritage site unique in the world.

Steam was raised again at the old pumping station at 2.20 pm on April 4, 1970 when Boulton and Watt's 1812 engine

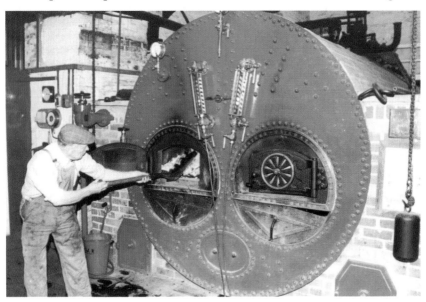

The boiler house

throbbed once more into life. The 1809 engine had been replaced with a new one from Harvey & Co., of Hayles, Cornwall in 1846 and it remains in use today. When the great engines are in steam, the pumping station is busy with volunteers to ensure that visitors miss no aspect of an operation of which they are demonstrably so proud.

A tour starts at the Boiler House with its enormous Lancashire boiler, 27 feet long and 7'3" in diameter.

Then it is along past a fascinating display or smaller working steam engines to the Driving Platform where an operator carefully regulates the steam pressure to ensure smooth running of the engine.

Two flights of stairs take you to the Beam Gallery the top storeyof which reveals the full majesty of the steam Leviathans which once powered the workshop of the world. Here the 26 foot long cast iron beams of the station's two steam engines are supported by a massive central wall which carries the working loads of the engines down into the foundations of the building. The Boulton and Watt beam weighs six tons and the beam of the second, Harvey engine, weighs 41/2 tons. This second engine was bought as part of an effort to improve the efficiency of the pumping station as the fierce winds of competition began to blow hard from the direction of the railways, ironically a competitor only made possible by steam power.

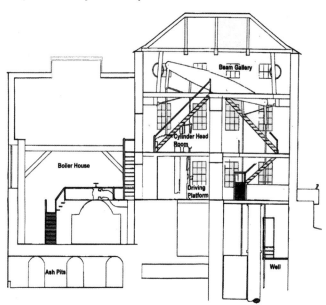

A flight of wooden stairs brings you down to the Cylinder Head Room where visitors can begin to appreciate the power generated by the great engines as the piston rod is driven downwards on the power stroke.

A railway, once part of the Great Western, still runs close to the pumping station as a graphic reminder of what ended the age of canals. Not far away is a major highway of the kind which ended the manic phase of the age of rail. In 1852, the Great Western Railway Company purchased the Kennet and Avon Canal but agreed not to close it and the pumping station remained active until 1958 when its steam engines were finally retired. British Waterways, the new owners of the Canal, continued the task of raising water using first diesel and then electric pumps.

On April 14, 1968, the Crofton Pumping Station was purchased for £75 by the Kennet and Avon Canal Trust with the object of restoring it to full working order. It is the results of over three decades of enthusiastic restoration, operation and maintenance that visitors are privileged to see today, almost two centuries after the pumping station first began its long and unique life of service to Britain's waterways.

**Please telephone for opening
times and admission charges or
consult the web site**

**Crofton, Marlborough,
Wiltshire
SN8 3DW
(Off A4 or A338)
Tel: 01672 870300
www.katrust.org**

MUSEUM OF THE GREAT WESTERN RAILWAY

Kemble Drive, Swindon, Wiltshire SN2 2TA
Tel: 01793 466646 Fax: 01793 466615 Textphone: 01793 466618
www.steam-museum.org.uk

T o enter STEAM, The Museum of the Great Western Railway at Swindon, is to enter a 'world', rather like the 'worlds' at Disneyland.

Often in original buildings, the 'world' of the Great Western Railway and of the men and women who built and operated it for more than a century is brought so vividly to life that it is easy to imagine we are actually there.

Unlike no other British railway, the Great Western was conceived by the flamboyant and energetic Isambard Kingdom Brunel in designer terms. He saw it not as a copy of schemes already built or under construction but as a whole new railway system, with its own unique buildings, track, track gauge and motive power.

Brunel was very much a man of his time, a time when a flood of new inventions inspired the brave to unimaginable feats. In Brunel's case it would involve attempting to build a tunnel under the River Thames and plans to throw a bridge across the Avon Gorge at Bristol. While in Bristol recovering his

health after being trapped in floods which swept through the Thames tunnel, Brunel was selected to build a railway from Bristol to London. It was 1833 and the era of railway mania had begun.

Brunel rode, on horseback, the 112 miles from Bristol to London many times to identify the best route for the Great Western, and when work commenced he threw himself into its direction and supervision 20 hours-a-day. Brunel was talented, ambitious and oriented toward profit. His was very much a case of seize the day. Railways inspired and excited Brunel to the point where even his honeymoon was spent surveying sites for new railways.

Many of the structures Brunel built have become monuments to the railway era and can still be visited today - from Temple Meads Station in Bristol to Paddington Station in London, along the way including Maidenhead Bridge over the Thames and the Royal Albert Bridge across the River Tamar at Saltash

The route of the Great Western includes Box Tunnel, longer than any other built at the time and costing the lives of a hundred workmen. Seven tunnels, four bridges and two viaducts, one of seventy three arches leading into Bath Station, were required to complete the line. Eventually, the railway would employ an incredible 70,000 people, 12,000 in the railway's bureaucracy and many of these women.

Brunel and others charged with operating the new line gradually realized that they needed their own works at which to service the locomotives, carriages and trucks bought into the system. Adequate land availability in Bristol or London

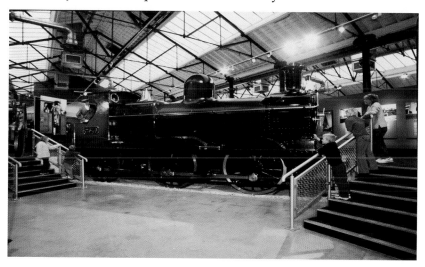

would be problematical and expensive but a green field site somewhere strategic in between would be ideal.

Today, you visit the Great Western Railway Museum at Swindon because this was the location chosen for a repair and maintenance works, at the junction of the Cheltenham branch line and at the place where it was planned to change locomotives on Bristol-London trains in preparation for the difficult westward haul up gradients which could reach 1 in a 100 at the Box Tunnel and the Bassett Incline.

The new site was just outside the old town of Swindon and lacked all infrastructure, including houses for workers. But the very fact that it was a pristine location made it ideal for the Great Western's planners.

Virtually from the start, it was realized that what could be repaired could also be built and within three short years Swindon was building its own locomotives, beginning appropriately enough with 'The Great Western.'

In 1868, a carriage and wagon works was opened and with modernizations and additions along the way, especially the building of the huge 'A' Erecting Shop, Swindon became one of the biggest and best equipped railway workshops in the world, covering an area of 326 acres, 73 of them roofed. The 'A' Erecting Shop was the place where the locomotive jigsaw was finally completed and all the components put in place.

During World war II, the works supported the war effort through the manufacture of shell and bomb cases, tanks, landing craft and midget submarines. For the first time, women worked in every part of the works.

British Railway's last steam locomotive, the 'Evening Star' was built at Swindon in 1960. In 1963 a large part of the carriage works' was closed. With the end of diesel locomotive production, the works days were clearly numbered and it closed its doors for the last time in 1986.

The entrance of the 'STEAM' Museum is part of the original Brunel works and the main exhibition area was one of a series of Machine Shops located around the works. To the rear, the Works Managers Offices have become the headquarters of the National Monuments Record Centre and, in front, the old Boiler Shop complex has become the Great Western Designer Outlet Village.

Inside the Museum, visitors can see examples of the great warriors of steam which once hauled goods and people between London and Bristol, in the process, opening up whole areas of the West Country to modern tourism, only to be superseded when cheap air travel made holidays abroad more attractive.

The mighty locomotives on display at the Museum begin with the 0-6-0 'Dean Goods' built in 1897 and the oldest engine in the collection. There are locomotive exhibits or designs by all the works' leading locomotive superintendents, including the 'King George V,' built in 1927 as the flagship of the Great Western Railway.

In the same way that the engines were awesome, the most highly prized, glamorous and skilled job was that of engine driver. Even those who did the dirty work of keeping the great Goliath's shining and spotless took a pride in their work we can hardly imagine

today. There are two hands-on exhibits in the Museum so you can have a go at driving yourself.

In addition to train crews, many thousands of other employees kept the train wheels rolling and life-like exhibits show dress and working conditions ranging from the girls in the components stock rooms, through office staff to engineers, mechanics and fitters. There is even a foreman looking grumpily at his watch as an employee arrives late for work - looking suitably concerned.

Displays incorporating the humble but utilitarian freight wagon up to the luxury express allow visitors almost to participate in a world long gone. You can wait at the railway station, see what it was like to take refreshments and even experience the lonely days of the signal man in his box as he kept the trucks and carriages moving along the increasingly busy lines.

Those fascinated by the back room work of Britain's unique and colourful railway history can see some of the lathes, drills, grinders, planers and slotters once belt driven by stationary steam engines and which were used to manufacture and repair the railway's rolling stock. They can see how axleboxes, bogies, brake gear, door handles and even luggage rack nets were made in the Carriage Body Shop. And they can see the mahogany and teak frame of a typical post-First World War carriage being prepared to take its steel cladding.

Of course, a railway is not only rolling stock but also station furniture, ticket machines, hand carts and even the posters produced to lure the excited public to travel to destinations as exotic as the English Riviera. No other railway in Britain matched the quality and output of the Great western's publicity materials.

When you pass through the doors of STEAM you are literally entering the world of the Great Western Railway as it was once upon a time. This very special Museum is open all year round, has an excellent cafe overlooking the main entrance and a well-stocked gift shop selling railway memorabilia, books and videos.

Ironbridge Gorge
World Heritage Site

Photo © The Ironbridge Gorge Museums

The names of Abraham Darby and Coalbrookdale reverberate throughout the Industrial Revolution as virtually no others. And it is for this reason that the Ironbridge Gorge in which Coalbrookdale is located and Darby carried out his experiments has been recognized by UNESCO as a World Heritage Site.

Darby pioneered the use of coke to smelt iron, freeing the iron industry from its traditional dependence on charcoal and Britain's dwindling forests.

By enabling coke iron smelting Darby's revolutionary process led eventually to an explosion in the use of cast-iron. Iron became the material of everything from pots and pans to bridges, buildings, locomotives, ships, guns, machines and tools, spawning entire new industries and creating whole new towns. Meanwhile, the demand for coal to make coke led to the opening up of new mining districts and the establishment of new industrial communities in what were once rural areas.

Areas close to coal, where iron making was carried on - places like Birmingham, West Bromwich, Walsall and Sheffield in the Midlands and the North of England, Newcastle in the North East, Liverpool in the North West and the great Carron Ironworks, near Edinburgh in Scotland developed into metal products manufactures for Britain and for the world.

Abraham Darby I was not a native of Coalbrookdale but moved there from Bristol in his search for a way of replacing expensive brass in the production of household metal pots and utensils. He had set up an iron foundry in Bristol in 1703 when he was only twenty five and travelling in Europe he had been struck by the advantages of casting molten metal in sand moulds with a metal cheaper than brass. He even imported Dutch experts to Bristol but the Grail of discovering the way to smelt iron of a quality high enough to make kitchen pots eluded them.

Meanwhile, at the turn of the 18th century the need to find a substitute for charcoal in iron smelting had turned into a positive clamour and there were many who claimed to have discovered a way of using less expensive coke, claims

Abraham Darby's furnace in which he smelted cast iron using coke instead of charcoal - in the grounds of the Museum of Iron.

unfortunately always unsubstantiated. The sulphur in most coal made the iron too brittle.

If Darby could find a way of producing high quality cast- iron cheaply, using coke, he could realize his dream of producing inexpensive iron frying pans, cooking pots and other utensils.

The story goes that a Welsh apprentice of Darby's at Bristol, John Thomas, showed him the secret. The boy was sworn to silence and put under contract to tell no one for three years.

If excessive sulphur remained a problem with

Thomas's process, it would have been natural for Darby to think about Coalbrookdale up-river from Bristol on the busy River Severn. At Coalbrookdale, the coal was known to be low in sulphur and therefore eminently suitable for use in the blast furnaces.

Coalbrookdale, which in the 18th century was synonymous with the area now known as Ironbridge Gorge, was a famous industrial region and would have been known to Darby even at his family home in nearby Dudley. In any case other Bristol Quakers already had a brassworks there. Also, Darby had served an apprenticeship in the growing metal working district of Birmingham, south of both Dudley and Coalbrookdale. Iron furnaces had operated at Coalbrookdale at least since 1545 and coal had also been mined in the area since Tudor times.

Darby moved from Bristol to Coalbrookdale in 1708 with John Thomas in tow. He leased and repaired a disused 17th century charcoal furnace and began to experiment with coked coal as a fuel.

UNUSUALLY STRONG

His blast furnace was unusually large and his blast unusually strong. Darby's stronger blast was made possible by Thomas Newcomen's invention of the atmospheric beam engine in 1708 which enabled the iron master to pump a stronger head of water for the wheel which worked the bellows of the blast furnace. Newcomen was from Dartmouth, Devon, but his engine first operated at Dudley Castle, Staffordshire, where it was used to pump water from a colliery. Within one year, his blast assisted by Newcomen's engine, Darby had successfully smelted cast-iron using coke.

The coke-smelting process was slow to catch on because it applied only to cast-iron and not to wrought-iron. At first, coke could only be used in the production of cast-iron because coke-smelted pig iron produced bar iron of inferior quality to that made from charcoal pig. Nevertheless, The range of cast-iron articles increased steadily, eventually threatening the

The upper part of Blists Hill Victorian Town

dominance of wrought- iron and offering strong competition to brass, copper, lead and wood. As he had dreamed, during his lifetime, Darby was indeed able to sell his iron pots and pans to customers along the Severn and at markets throughout the Midlands.

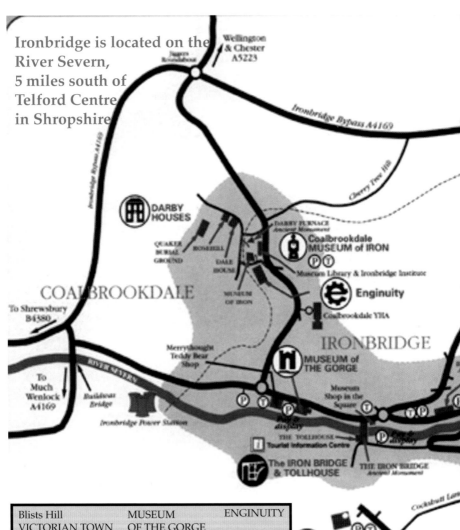

Ironbridge is located on the River Severn, 5 miles south of Telford Centre in Shropshire

Wellington & Chester A5223

Ironbridge Bypass A4169

Cherry Tree Hill

DARBY HOUSES

DARBY FURNACE
Ancient Monument

QUAKER BURIAL GROUND

ROSEHILL

DALE HOUSE

Coalbrookdale MUSEUM of IRON

Museum Library & Ironbridge Institute

COALBROOKDALE

MUSEUM OF IRON

Enginuity

To Shrewsbury B4380

Coalbrookdale YHA

Merrythought Teddy Bear Shop

IRONBRIDGE

MUSEUM of THE GORGE

To Much Wenlock A4169

RIVER SEVERN

Buildwas Bridge

Museums Shop in the Square

Ironbridge Power Station

THE TOLLHOUSE
Tourist Information Centre

The IRON BRIDGE & TOLLHOUSE

THE IRON BRIDGE
Ancient Monument

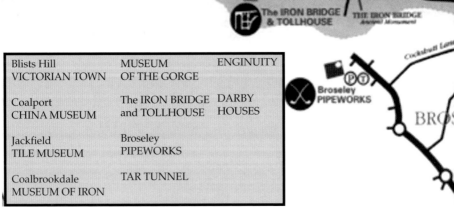

Blists Hill VICTORIAN TOWN	MUSEUM OF THE GORGE	ENGINUITY
Coalport CHINA MUSEUM	The IRON BRIDGE and TOLLHOUSE	DARBY HOUSES
Jackfield TILE MUSEUM	Broseley PIPEWORKS	
Coalbrookdale MUSEUM OF IRON	TAR TUNNEL	

Cockshutt Lane

Broseley PIPEWORKS

BRO

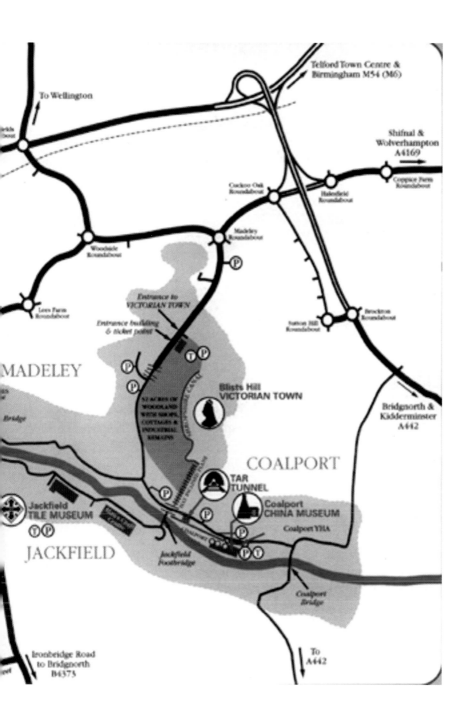

It would take another forty years of experimentation and improvement before Darby's process was fully perfected by his son, also called Abraham, who in 1750, with the help of the Cranage Brothers, managed to smelt pig iron with coke and produce wrought- iron. At last, industry had a way of producing wrought-iron on a large scale using cheap coke. Within four years, Coalbrookdale had seven furnaces at work with five Newcomen engines. John Smeaton's invention of the compressed air pump and especially of double acting, steam-powered, blowing cylinders tolled the final death knell for charcoal and assured the supremacy of coke.

Darby's grandson, Abraham Darby III took over the Coalbrookdale works just at a time when he could capitalize on all the earlier developments and his iron bridge across the River Severn reflects the explosive exuberance felt at the time about the use of iron which, as in the case of canals and railways, was destined to become a mania throughout the land.

Throughout the 18th century, the Severn was a major artery of transport and trade connecting Gloucester with Welshpool. In 1758, some 400 vessels were recorded as using the river for trade and by the turn of the century the number had doubled. The Severn Gorge was not only home to Coalbrookdale and its ironworks but also to a host of other industries ranging from primary coal, clay and ironstone mines to works producing bricks, tiles, pottery and clay products. The quiet gorge was often wreathed in smoke by day and lit with the red fires of furnaces by night. By day, noise and clatter were everywhere and at night the many local inns and taverns provided light relief to the bargees and labourers from the grime and ardours of the river, mine or factory.

Today, the archaeological corridor of Blists Hill occupies the site of former coal mining, iron making and brick and tile works as well as part of the Shropshire Canal with its audacious Hay Inclined Plane - still a marvel of ingenuity and open to the public. The Canal terminated here and the Hay Inclined Plane was built in 1792 to allow tub-boats to move quickly from one level to another. There were also numerous rail

The world-famous Iron Bridge

and plateways connecting the mines, ironworks, forges and manufactures to each other and to the Severn. What is known today as the Tar Tunnel was built in 1786 to give mines at Blists Hill direct access to the river. A spring of natural bitumen was struck during construction which came to be used for pitch, fuel oil and medicinal preparations. The tunnel still oozes bitumen today.

At Blists Hill during the past 30 years a small town has been created with rebuilt cottages and workshops, crafts and trades and a wealth of events which reflect life at the end of the 19th century. Visitors can chat to the townsfolk about Victorian industry, crafts, customs and traditions. At the bank, money can be exchanged for "Victorian" tokens to spend in the shops or to enjoy a drink at the New Inn Public House.

Across the River severn, Brosely had been known for its clay products since the 16th century, especially clay pipes, and modern visitors can drop into the Brosely Pipeworks where it seems as if the workers have just popped out for a break.

Pipes were not the only items to be made from clay. At nearby Jackfield, the decorative tile industry would expand to include the two largest factories in the world, one of them, the Craven Dunnil Tile Works, now housing a unique museum which is an Aladdin's Cave of ceramic fascination. The encaustic tile works of Maw & Co., is now a crafts centre and can be reached either by car or by means of a short and very pleasant canal side walk from the Coalport China Museum, on the north bank of the Severn.

Coalport, now the site of the Coalport China Museum,was opened in 1796 by 24-year-old John Rose and destined to become one of the largest porcelain producers in the world, eventually being bought by the Wedgwood Group in 1967. The Museum displays some of the products made at Coalport as well as illustrating the way of life of the china makers. The mysteries of their art can be unravelled in workshops, hands-on activities and at demonstrations.

The industrial realities of Ironbridge Gorge in the late 18th century are brought vividly to life by a giant model at the old Severn Warehouse, now the Museum of the Gorge. The model took many years to research and six months to construct and represents one day in the history of Coalbrookdale, the occasion of the visit of the Prince of Orange, Stadtholder Willem V and his wife on August 12, 1796.

OVERCOME BOTTLENECK

Numerous ferry crossings were required on the busy Severn to carry the raw materials of burgeoning industry as well as its growing workforce. With ferries plying to and fro and trows or sailing barges navigating up and down the river there must certainly have been times when the narrow gorge was massively congested causing irritating and costly delays.

It wasn't Darby's idea to build a new bridge but with coach and cart traffic growing rapidly using improved roads the need to overcome the bottleneck at the Gorge must have been great and constantly increasing. Darby was so keen to be able to build the bridge in iron rather than stone or wood that he agreed to fund any overspend himself and eventually had to fork out £3,000. The furnaces at Coalbrookdale even had to be enlarged to make the 378 tons of iron required. The bridge opened in 1781 with tolls being collected continuously until 1950 when the bridge passed into the ownership of Shropshire County Council. The Iron Bridge and the tollhouse can still be seen and, indeed, the iconography of the bridge has become famous around the world.

The ribs of the Iron Bridge were joined together by means of iron mortises and tenons just as if they were made of wood and the load bearing capability of the slender yet strong struts soon provided provenance for uses ranging from ship's hulls to the pillars which would soon support the brick cladding of the age's new, fire proof, factories the first of which was built at nearby Shrewsbury in 1796 and can still be seen today known as the Maltings. In its way, the Iron Bridge, can be claimed as the true ancestor of the modern skyscraper.

Ironbridge is almost equally famous for Abraham Darby I and the coke smelting of iron as for Abraham Darby III and the building of the Iron Bridge across the Severn. But Ironbridge Gorge as a whole is much more even than this. The recognition as a World Heritage Site of what was once called "the most extraordinary district in the world" was given because, like no other place on earth, Ironbridge Gorge is a living museum of the beginnings of industry which transformed our daily lives on this planet. The first iron railway wheels were made here, the first cast-iron steam engine cylinders, the first iron rails. Visitors came to Ironbridge from all over the world to marvel at the new technologies. Artists came to paint and sketch the revolutionary scenes of life, landscape and industry.

In the hilly landscape around the Gorge you can still see early ironworking furnaces and forges and revolutionary transport and power systems next to ironmaster's houses, workers' homes, warehouses, churches and chapels, schools and workshops. The first Abraham Darby's residence at Dale House, overlooking Coalbrookdale is open to visitors as is the nearby

Darby family home, Rosehill. Tragically, Abraham Darby I died before he could move in to his beautiful new home. Dale House was lived in by five generations of Darby's family and displays show how it would have been in the 1850s. Abraham Darby III lived here while planning the construction of the Iron Bridge.

In 1700 Coalbrookdale had consisted of five houses, a furnace and a forge or two. By 1740 there was housing and employment for close to 500 people. By 1851 Coalbrookdale was the largest iron foundry in the world employing 3,000 people. By then, the company specialized in fine art castings including statues, staircases, balconies, balustrades, fountains fireplaces, fluted columns as well as every kind of domestic necessity practical to render in iron. Many examples of these products can be seen in the Museum of Iron at Coalbrookdale.

Many of the families attracted to Coalbrookdale were squatters but a few were able to live in company houses. Examples of these homes, vividly illustrating the lifestyle, can be seen at Blists Hill. What cannot now be seen is the dirt and disease in which many of these newcomers lived, not only on land but on the boats and barges moored on the Severn. Cholera was endemic and Abraham Darby I died of typhoid at the age of 39.

The ten museums of Ironbridge Gorge are each very different, providing unique insights into life and times long past in ways interesting and entertaining for modern visitors curious about their industrial past or just wanting an enjoyable day out with a difference. Some museums have tea and coffee shops, retail outlets and car parking and a passport is available for entrance to multiple sites.

Enginuity, the newest and most interactive attraction at Coalbrookdale, follows a 300-year tradition of inspiring amazing engineering and technology. Visitors can find out how to pull a locomotive, control water to generate electricity, test their speed and accuracy against a robot or work as a team to make the Crazy Boiler blow its top - all very much in the tradition of the Darby's and of Coalbrookdale.

Photo©DJ Houlston Photography

Traditional tile making continues today within the World Heritage Site

For museum opening times and admission charges please contact:

Tel: 01952 432166 or 01952 433522. Fax: 01952 432166
Groups: 01952 433522
Email: visits@ironbridge.org.uk
Education & school visits: 01952 433970
Email: education@ironbridge.org.uk
www.ironbridge.org.uk or www.ironbridge.ws

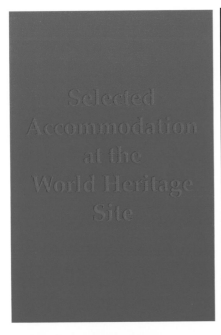

Selected Accommodation at the World Heritage Site

Coalbrookdale Villa

Paradise,
Telford,
Shropshire
TF8 7NR
Tel:01952 433450.

Website: www.coalbrookdalevilla.co.uk
Contact June Ashdown

A large Victorian Gothic-style ironmaster's house located just off the main Wharfage in Ironbridge - minutes away from the town and major museums in the Gorge. No need to take the car! To an ideal location can be added a warm welcome, en suite rooms, relaxing gardens and ample parking.

Photo: © Telford & Wrekin Council

100

101

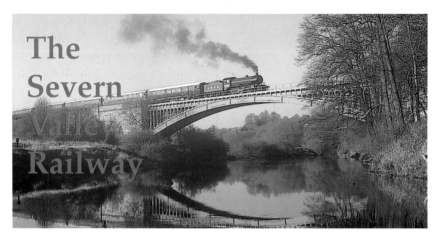

The Severn Valley Railway

The Severn Valley Railway runs for 16 miles from Bridgnorth in Shropshire to Kidderminster in Worcestershire and boasts one of the largest collections of steam locomotives and coaches, including rolling stock which is over 80 years old. It hosts many special events throughout the year including visits by those children's favourites "Thomas the Tank Engine" and of course "Santa". Other events include the popular "1940s Weekend", "Classic Car and Bike Day" and "Severn Valley in Bloom."

The beautiful valley of the River Severn is best seen from the train or by alighting at one of the intermediate stations you can enjoy a walk along the riverside paths.

The Railway offers a wide variety of catering facilities ranging from the buffets at the main stations, a trolley service on the trains, through to the ever-popular Sunday luncheon trains which operate on most Sundays throughout the year and for which advance booking is required.

World's First Fireproof Factory

The world's very first multi-storey fire proof factory is difficult to find. It is not a World Heritage Site and indeed has no connection yet with any of the industrial heritage sites to which thousands flock yearly to find out more about Britain's proud industrial past. Yet it does exist.

The man who invented the fire proof factory was Charles Bage who moved to Shrewsbury in 1780. Shrewsbury was a regional market, a finishing centre for woollens and a town of drapers.

New inventions in spinning set men thinking about new designs for the mills which would house them.

Shrewsbury's woollen industry was in decline yet the town had 5,000 workers, many skilled in finishing textiles and there were handloom weavers in the surrounding villages.

Shrewsbury entrepreneurs Thomas and Benjamin Beynon and John Marshall of Leeds combined to build a new mill at Ditherington, just north of Shrewsbury Castle. The new mill would be at the cutting edge of technology relying not on water power but on the new steam engines being made by Boulton and Watt at Birmingham. The first engines were ordered in 1796 when the building of the mills commenced. Bage was a minor partner in the venture.

He had already produced a design for a modern mill which he outlined in a letter to William Strutt that very same year, the design based on the earliest known practical theory for the strength of cast iron columns. The Ditherington sponsors were impressed. Thanks to developments at nearby Coalbrookdale iron mania was sweeping the country. In 1796, a large iron foundry was opened at Wyle

The interior of Ditherington Flax Mill.

in Shrewsbury. With Bage's suggestions accepted, the iron columns, roof trusses and beams which would be used at Ditherington instead of wood were all cast conveniently in this local foundry.

The new mill opened in 1797 having been completed at record speed in less than 12 months. The world's first multi-storey fire proof factory had arrived.

Today, the mill still stands and is under renovation. But sometime soon, the public will once again be able to see samples of Bage's work, an accomplishment which led directly to the iconic North American skyscraper.

Based on information kindly supplied by Michael J. King.

The Wedgwood Story

The Wedgwood Visitor Centre,
Barlaston,
Stoke-on-Trent,
Staffordshire ST12 9ES.
Tel: 01782 282986
www.thewedgwoodvisitorcentre.com

OPEN ALL YEAR

Image by courtesy of the Wedgwood Museum Trust,
Barlaston, Staffordshire.

Engraving of the ' Churchyard' Works - the site of Josiah Wedgwood I's birth in July 1730.

The pristine greenfield site at Barlaston, just outside Stoke-on-Trent, with its tree lined drives, verdant lawns and modern buildings provides a surprising setting for those in search of the historical Josiah Wedgwood I.

There is not a hint of the soot encrusted red brick factory one expects, nor any sign of the smoke belching bottle ovens once so evocative of the Potteries.

Yet from the moment the curious visitor first glimpses Wedgwood's bronze statue outside the Barlaston factory, the master potter posed intently examining a copy of his famous Portland Vase, one feels the presence of the man and of his world.

The history of the man who virtually invented

Preceding page image: Portrait of Josiah Wedgwood I (1730-95), oil on canvas, painted in 1782 by Sir Joshua Reynolds.

Image by courtesy of the Wedgwood Museum Trust, Barlaston, Staffordshire.
Engraving of the 'Brick House' also known as 'Bell' Works.

Britain's modern pottery industry by bringing order to factory production can be seen in a remarkable permanent exhibition at Barlaston known appropriately as 'The Wedgwood Story'.

'The Wedgwood Story' is much more than an exhibition, as the present Lord Wedgwood makes clear in his introduction to the Visitor Centre printed in an attractive and informative guide: "For our Wedgwood Story we have taken much time and great care to make

Image by courtesy of the Wedgwood Museum Trust, Barlaston, Staffordshire.

Engraving of the ' Ivy House' Works, Burslem. It was here that Wedgwood commenced business on his own account on May Day, 1759.

this a tour like no other. The Company's rich heritage is beautifully illustrated with film, rare exhibits and interactive displays. The tour follows the entire production process from raw clay to throwing, forming and casting, glazing, firing and decorating. It reveals a continuing tradition of superb craftsmanship and shows how the vision and brilliance of one man in the 18th century lives on, hand in hand with the finest technology of today."

Lord Wedgwood puts film at the top of his list of visitor "must sees." A twenty minute film plunges the visitor into the ambience of Josiah's world and quickly and entertainingly reveals the events which culminated in Wedgwood's worldwide recognition as a leader and entrepreneur who revolutionised Britain's pottery industry. After the film, the displays feature some examples of the Company's most famous creations enhanced by audio visuals. A factory tour shows how modern Wedgwood is made today and the visitor can buy contemporary Wedgwood

Group of late 18th century Jasper, showing some of the range of colours available during the lifetime of the founder of the Wedgwood Company, Josiah I. Date circa 1785-90.

ware from on site shops at prices suitable for all.

Born in 1730, Josiah

Wedgwood I lived in exciting times. Population was increasing rapidly, raising the demand for every kind of consumer goods from clothes through to pottery. New and sometimes higher incomes were being created outside the traditional agricultural sector. Foreign trade was also booming as Britain supplied the world with finished goods. The young Wedgwood found himself at the centre of this storm of change and quickly realized the potential for commercial opportunities.

The rich had been importing expensive porcelain from Europe and China for decades. Wedgwood saw not only a chance to replace these with locally produced wares but also to supply the burgeoning "middle class" market, by replacing expensive plate, and cheaper wood, pewter and coarse wares with serviceable and affordable ceramics. He was helped substantially by the growing mania for the drinking of tea! He was an ambitious man who dreamt of conquering foreign markets and becoming 'Potter to the Universe.'

Wedgwood was the fourth generation of a family of potters, clever at school and electrified by the new possibilities, not only in the market place but in the craft of pottery making itself. Dotted around the Staffordshire countryside were more than 150 potteries, virtually cottage industries, where a few craftsmen turned out coarse ware for local markets. Far from being able to take advantage of the new possibilities, the industry was in decline! This was Wedgwood's challenge!

A local Master Potter, Thomas Whieldon, saw Wedgwood's potential and in 1754 took him on as a junior partner. Wedgwood worked tirelessly, commencing experiments which would eventually revolutionise the local industry.

Within five years and by the time he was twenty eight , Wedgwood had enough money to set up on his own account at the 'Ivy House' works rented from his uncles in the town of his birth, Burslem. The achievement in moving to the 'Ivy House' clearly demonstrated that Wedgwood was no mere technician but an entrepreneur of the new breed, with an eye for opportunity, able to secure capital, select a site for a works, plan, forecast and manage workers and production - no easy matters in the years before factory routines and discipline were firmly established. Later, his Etruria Works would be a model of new factory organization and its staff management and surrounding housing complex a reflection of the progressive manner in which Wedgwood thought the men and women who worked for him should be treated. Within a few years the 'Ivy House' works proved to be too small and Wedgwood moved to larger premises, the 'Brick House' Works, Burslem. These were also known as the 'Bell' works because of Josiah's innovative use of a bell to summon employees to work.

The first product to begin to make Wedgwood's name a household one was his new cream coloured earthenware, which was to take British and overseas markets virtually by storm. The mistress of any house who once saw it, wanted to buy it - including King George III's consort, Queen Charlotte. Her Royal patronage in 1765 enabled Josiah to call his creamware 'Queen's Ware'and to style himself 'Potter to her Majesty.'

Wedgwood's development of his new Queen's Ware body was to make his name internationally famous but in order to fuel publicity still further he undertook a succession of high profile commissions for the rich and famous, including Royalty.

Perhaps the most famous commission in Queen's Ware was a 952 piece dinner and dessert service ordered by the Empress Catherine,' The Great' of Russia in 1773-74. Each of the pieces comprising the service featured 1,244 hand painted views of English mansions, gardens and geological phenomena.

The rich and famous were the leaders of fashion. Wedgwood calculated that what the great and the good would buy would soon be sought after by the middle class. His pursuit of the titled and the aristocratic was therefore the foundation of his marketing strategy. It also enabled him to charge higher prices than his competitors. Wedgwood streamlined his factory costs but did not believe in lowering prices. In his view, high prices were associated with high quality and Wedgwood desired to be known for his superior product.

Getting the new products to market from the landlocked Potteries was neither easy nor

Image by courtesy of the Wedgwood Museum Trust, Barlaston, Staffordshire.

First edition of the Portland (also known as Barberini) vase. White on black Jasper. Formerly in the collection of Thomas Hope, Antiquarian. Date 1793.

Image by courtesy of the Wedgwood Museum Trust, Barlaston, Staffordshire.

Queen's Ware (cream coloured earthenware) tureen, lid and stand, decorated with the 18th century border pattern known as ' Green Waterleaf'. Date circa 1780.

without substantial cost. The area was isolated and with few roads and no canals.

Railways had not yet been invented. Transporting pottery by pack horse meant that the cost of breakages was excessive. By 1763 Wedgwood was promoting the construction of a new turnpike road to link the Potteries with burgeoning colonial markets as well as to compete with traditional suppliers in Europe. Two years later he was actively promoting the building of a canal. One canal boat could carry a hundred times more than a packhorse and with fewer breakages!

In the mid-1760s, Wedgwood felt ready to expand again - this time to build a new works which he called Etruria - so named because at that time the Greek vases which were all the rage were thought to be Etruscan. The works was built alongside the Trent and Mersey Canal which, with the exception of a building known as the 'Round House', was sadly demolished in the 1960s.

At first, Wedgwood intended his new Etruria factory, which opened on June 13, 1769, to specialise in vessels with shapes and decoration based on recent finds of ancient pottery from archaeological sites such as Pompeii, in Italy. Later, his products would reflect whatever was in desirable in fashionable society. In 1768, Wedgwood both fascinated and appealed to his 'up-market' clientele by developing a fine ornamental black stoneware which he christened 'Black Basalt,' of classical dimensions with panels decorated in red enamel which compared favourably with its Etruscan prototypes.

By the mid-1770s, Wedgwood had developed his new and unique stoneware body which he named Jasper -, seen at its most exquisite in Wedgwood's limited edition Portland Vase, also known as 'Barberini.' The vase was a copy of a 1st century Roman glass original and became the hallmark of a line of blue, sea green and other products with white cameo bas relief figures which would become instantly recognisable as Wedgwood for all time.

Black Basalt and Jasper became the foundation of Wedgwood's ornamental wares. Wedgwood prized the new

Image by courtesy of The Wedgwood Visitor Centre, Barlaston, Staffordshire.

Visitors to the Wedgwood Story Visitor Centre at Barlaston can experience the whole production process from raw clay to throwing, forming and casting, glazing, firing and decorating.

Jasper body above all his former ceramic inventions. A vast range of ornamental items were evolved in this superior new ceramic material - even cameos were made in Jasper and were combined with precious metals and cut steel supplied by such prestigious manufacturers as Matthew Boulton of the Soho Works, Birmingham. Cameos were the first items produced in Jasper, with larger pieces such as vases, and tea wares coming much later.

Wedgwood sought not only the leaders of society and fashion as his key clients but anything of public interest, and therefore popular, which could be commemorated in ceramic form he was sure not to miss.

Wedgwood was closely associated with the iron master, Matthew Boulton and with steam king, James Watt, regularly attending meetings of the Lunar Society held at various venues in and around Birmingham. Like Lunar Society members, Wedgwood was at the very heart of the Industrial Revolution, introducing techniques and processes which were the foundation of modern factory and technical production. He was also an accomplished scientist and was elected a Fellow of the Royal Society for his invention of the thermometer, also known as the pyrometer, a device which for the first time enabled workmen to gauge the firing temperature of bottle ovens.The guesswork could now be taken out of this process.

The Master Potter was the most modern of men, a keen supporter of free trade, an ardent proponent of liberty and an implacable opponent of slavery. Wedgwood produced Jasper medallions of the American leaders Benjamin Franklin and George Washington at the time of the American Wars of Independence. His medallion featuring the emblem of the Abolition of Slavery Society, the kneeling, manacled slave surmounted by the legend: 'Am I not a man and a brother?'epitomised his philanthropy.

When Josiah died in 1795 he left an enduring legacy of quality. When the Wedgwood factory relocated from Etruria to its present Barlaston location in 1940, this electric-fired pottery was destined to be the most modern not only in Britain but in Europe.

Today, the Wedgwood Company's expert skills and innovative products continue to be built on the great legacy of the past, a legacy begun by a young man born almost three centuries ago, the twelth son of a mediocre potter who promised him a £20 inheritance which he never received. When he died, Wedgwood's name was known all over the world. He left a fortune of £500,000, a considerable sum in those days, had established the most up-to-date pottery in Europe and was a notable figure not only in the pottery industry but also in politics and science.

Wedgwood was described by the Victorian Prime Minister Gladstone as "the greatest man who ever, in any age or country, applied himself to the important work of uniting art with industry."

The Potteries

THE POTTERIES MUSEUM & ART GALLERY
Bethesda Street,
Hanley, Stoke-on-Trent ST1 3DW
Tel: 01782 232323
Email: museums@stoke.gov.uk

GLADSTONE POTTERY MUSEUM
Uttoxeter Road,
Longton, Stoke-on-Trent ST3 1PQ.
Tel: 01782 319232
Email: gladstone@stoke.gov.uk

ETRURIA INDUSTRIAL MUSEUM
Lower Bedford Street,
Etruria, Stoke-on-Trent ST4 7AF
Tel: 01782 233144
Email: museums@stoke-ccgov.uk

FORD GREEN HALL
Ford Green Road,
Smallthorne, Stoke-on-Trent ST6 1NG
Tel: 01782 233195
Email: ford.green.hall@stoke.gov.uk

WEBSITE:
www.stoke.gov.uk/museums

The Potteries Museum & Art Gallery

he Potteries Museum and Art Gallery tells the story of the people, products and landscape of the North Staffordshire Potteries, the only area in Britain to be so completely identified with one industry.

Its outstanding ceramics collection provides a comprehensive overview of the development of British pottery from the 16th century onwards.

The museum's unequalled holdings of ceramics have their origins in the competing collections of the individual pottery towns, which eventually came together as Stoke-on-Trent in 1910.

In 1956 a museum was built on the site of the old Bell Works Pottery in Hanley to house this magnificent collection. This was intended to be the first phase of a building programme, but it was not until 1979 that the present museum was opened to the public, enabling new displays and interpretation of all its collections, including local and natural history, archaeology, fine and decorative arts, and ceramics. In 1997 the museum's collections were *Designated* by the United Kingdom government as being of outstanding importance.

More than 5,000 individual pieces of pottery are displayed in the ceramics gallery. Highlights include 17th century slip-decorated earthenwares, 18th century white salt-glazed stonewares, Wedgwood ware, figures, Victorian bone china and 20th century industrial and studio ceramics. In 2002, the museum acquired a number of significant items from the former Minton Museum, including a life-sized peacock and monumental pieces of majolica. The displays concentrate on Staffordshire wares and their dominance of the British market but also include the largest collection of 20th century studio ceramics in Britain from potters across the United Kingdom.

Other galleries explore the changing landscape and habitats of the Potteries, archaeological material ranging from Neolithic finds to wasters excavated from local factory sites, and the life of the local community, which is brought up to date in the family-oriented *You're History* gallery. Stoke-on-Trent was the birth place of the aviation designer Reginald Mitchell, and his achievements are celebrated in the form of a Mk XVI Spitfire.

A regular programme of special exhibitions and events draws on both the museum's own collections, particularly visual arts, and material loaned from major collections elsewhere in the United Kingdom and abroad.

Etruria Industrial Museum

T he canal network was crucial to the develop
ment of the North Staffordshire pottery
industry. The Trent and Mersey Canal
opened up the Potteries to international trade and provided
access to materials. The Caldon Canal linked the Potteries with
the Churnet Valley and nearby limestone quarries. The Etruria
Industrial Museum sits at the junction of these two canals. It
comprises Jesse Shirley's Etruscan Bone and Flint Mill, a Visitor
Centre, and a complex of canal buildings.

The Etruscan Bone and Flint Mill is a Scheduled
Ancient Monument and Grade II* listed building. It is Britain's
sole surviving steam-powered potters' mill and was built for
Jesse Shirley by George Kirk of Etruria in 1856. It remained in
production until 1972, grinding flint and bone for the pottery
industry. The mill is of a similar design to that built by George
Kirk for Josiah Wedgwood at Etruria Hall. Indeed the name
"Etruscan" Bone and Flint Mill borrows from Wedgwood the
allusion to Etruria in Italy where classical pottery was produced.

The mill houses a rotative beam engine, the 'Princess,' which was probably manufactured in the 1820s by Bateman and Sherratt of Salford. It is one of the oldest engines still in use in situ in Britain today. The mill retains its original machinery, including grinding pans, bevel gears, brick blungers, settling arks, jaw crusher and small horizontal steam engine. Mill buildings include a flint calcining kiln and a boiler house with a coal-fired, 1903 Cornish-type boiler built by William Evans of Cliffe Vale.

The steam engine and machinery have been restored and brought back to use for demonstration. Steaming weekends take place during the summer and autumn months, offering visitors an opportunity to appreciate the sheer force of the engine and grinding machinery.

The Visitor Centre tells the story of the industries and communities of Etruria, together with the history of the mill itself, the Shirley family and their workforce. Etruria offers a

microcosm of the Potteries. Local industries included not only ceramics but iron and steel making, engineering, a gasworks, brickworks and a chemical plant, as well as the mill. Etruria was also home to a lively community, with shops, schools, chapels, pubs, a park, sports clubs and brass bands. North Staffordshire's first infirmary occupied a nearby site, while pottery workers emigrating to America embarked from Etruria Wharf. An interactive display has been designed with the needs of both families and schools in mind.

Once the banks of the canals were lined with busy factories. Now they are home to many forms of wildlife, wild flowers and aquatic plants. The area around the museum provides nesting sites for a variety of birds and waters edge cover for nesting ducks, water-fowl and water voles. Fresh water mussels have been found on the canal bed and kingfishers visit the area. Swans, Canada geese and herons feed on the canal and bats appear at dusk.

Gladstone
Pottery
Museum

The Gladstone Pottery Museum exists *"to preserve and present the way of life of the pottery worker of North Staffordshire"*. Housed in the last surviving complete Victorian 'Potbank' or pottery factory, it comprises a group of workshops, warehouses, engine house, four bottle ovens and an enamel kiln centred around a cobbled courtyard. This complex of industrial buildings forms the last complete pottery factory site from the era of coal fired bottle ovens - once part of the characteristic industrial landscape of the Potteries, now unique.

The Grade II* listed buildings date from 1780 to the 1950s and typify the medium sized pottery factories which employed the bulk of the city's ceramic workforce. Gladstone China Works was an "ordinary" factory, not a household name, and it is this that makes it so important to the city's heritage; it is the only survivor among the many potbanks which once mass-produced the everyday products used by millions of people across the globe.

A development trust was established in 1971 to save the site and the Gladstone Pottery Museum opened to the public in 1975, winning the Museum of the Year award the following year. In 1994 the Museum became part of Stoke-on-Trent's museum service.

The museum aims not only to safeguard and interpret the buildings and machinery, but also to preserve and present the skills on which the pottery industry was built. Live demonstrators bring skills such as throwing, slip-casting, flower-making and decorating to life. Visitors experience the life of the pottery worker of North Staffordshire through first person interpretation. All aspects of the pottery-making process are illustrated within the complex of factory buildings.

Gladstone's unique collections of sanitary-ware and ceramic tiles are housed in two new galleries. The Tile Gallery looks at the history of tile-making from the mediaeval period to the present, and includes breath-taking examples of 19th and 20th century decorated tiles, together with a NASA space shuttle tile. *Flushed With Pride,* the sanitaryware gallery, tells the story of the toilet – and the crucial role of Stoke-on-Trent in its development.

Pottery work was unhealthy, a theme that is explored in the Doctor's house, once the home of a Certifying Surgeon, whose job was to visit local factories to examine workers for diseases such as lead poisoning. A Victorian surgery has been recreated, telling the story of healthcare in the polluted Potteries through a series of stark case-histories.

The enamel kiln is one of only two remaining in the city. Enamel firing is the final production process of pottery manufacture, when decorated ware is fired for the last time. This kiln, which is much smaller than the more familiar bottle ovens, has recently been restored and opened up, enabling the museum to display the complete process of pottery manufacture from the days of coal-fired bottle ovens.

Ford Green Hall

F ord Green Hall is a
timber - framed farmhouse with
18th century brick extensions.
The house was built in 1624 by the Ford
family. The building is listed Grade II* and
the grounds include an 18th century dovecote
and recreated period garden with herbs and a
viewing mount. The museum interprets the
pre-industrial history of Stoke-on-Trent
through the building and period room
settings which contain a designated collection
of furniture, textiles and ceramics. There is a
lively events programme throughout the year
and the museum has an award winning
education service and is licensed for
weddings.

Black Country Living Museum

DUDLEY

STOKE 974

DOCK C°

Tipton Road, Dudley, West Midlands DY1 4SQ

For opening times and admission charges:
Tel: 0121 557 9643
www.bclm.co.uk
info@bclm.co.uk
Group and educational bookings:
0121 520 8054

A replica of the world's first steam engine

Without the invention of steam power the pace of Britain's Industrial Revolution would have been vastly different. Once invented, steam powered engines led to rapid and spectacular developments in fuel extraction, manufacture and transport.

The fuel needed to power the new steam engines was coal and Staffordshire was lucky enough to be located on top of multiple seams of 'Thick Coal' with almost no partings or rock between them and often within only a few feet of the surface.

Coal came to be used to smelt first iron and subsequently steel. With malleable iron and high-strength steel came a flood of new products as well as the tools and machines with which to make them. Coal, steam and iron formed the foundation upon which workshops and factories mushroomed throughout the early 19th century.

In the Black Country, thousands of chimneys and furnaces filled the air with smoke, and the mining of the coal, ironstone, fireclay and limestone turned the ground inside out, creating large expanses of dereliction.

Canals were cut to transport the heavy and increasingly plentiful goods of the Black Country. The 26 acre Black Country Living Museum at Dudley is surrounded on three sides by canals and the Museum Village is built around the Dudley Tunnel Branch of the Birmingham Wolverhampton Canal. Electric powered canal boats take visitors on trips through the tunnel and deep into the spectacular limestone caverns.

But long before the age of canals it was the invention of steam power which propelled forward the Industrial Revolution.

The world's very first successful steam engine was built by Thomas Newcomen in 1712 and used to pump water from coal mines on the estates of Lord Dudley.

Based on an engraving dated 1719, the Black Country Museum has succeeded in building a replica of this engine.

The 'Fire Engine,' as it is known, is housed in a brick building from which a wooden beam projects through one wall. Rods hang from the outer end of the beam and operate the pumps which raise the water to the surface from the bottom of the mine shaft. In full steam, the massive engine, literally as big as a house, is an impressive site.

The ground beneath the Museum was once mined for the coal, limestone, fireclay and ironstone for which the region is famous. More than 40 mine shafts are shown on old plans and around one of these shafts, appropriately enough not far from the

A glimpse of life underground for man and horse.

Newcomen Engine, Racecourse Colliery has been built as a typical Black Country coal pit. The original shaft beneath the pit-frame was 120 feet deep. It is a drift mine, with a sloping tunnel down which visitors can walk safely to enter the lives of miners long ago.

Once underground, 'lija Wedge, a miner of the 1850s, leads visitors through the maze of timber-lined tunnels. He tells how boys started work at the age of 10 or 11, in a cold, damp job opening air doors which directed the air around the pit to prevent gas collecting and causing explosives. Miners can be seen, sometimes dangerously beneath the coal, cutting and hacking with only a simple pick axe. The sound and shake of blasting at the rock and the roar as tons of coal fall from the roof are reminders of the further dangers faced by the sturdy miners. Black Country pitsconcentrated on producing large lumps of coal which were packed onto trolleys and held together with iron bands for transporting to the pit bottom and then to the surface.

Historic buildings from all around the Black Country have been moved and rebuilt at the Museum to create an old-fashioned canal-side village - a fitting tribute to the traditional skills and enterprise of the people who once lived and worked in the heart of industrial Britain.

COSTUMED CHARACTERS

The Black Country Museum is a Living Museum and visitors therefore meet costumed characters in the original shops, houses and workshops, ride on a tramcar, visit the horses or watch classic comedies in the 1920s cinema. There is something to suit all tastes, from sweet-making and glass-cutting to the metal working which made the names of the Black Country and Birmingham known around the world. You can even sample fish and chips from a 1930s Fried Fish Shop and wash the meal down with a glass of real ale or dandelion and burdock from the Bottle and Glass Inn.

There is a programme of regular demonstrations and activities at the Museum, a range of meals and snacks available at several locations and a wealth of gifts and souvenirs to buy.

SOHO HOUSE

Soho House, Birmingham, reflects the wealth and opulence to which Matthew Boulton's ingenuity and business success eventually allowed him to aspire. The house has been faithfully restored to its 18th century elegance and Boulton lived there with his family from 1766 to 1809.

Like many successful men of his day, Matthew Boulton used his dining room with its mahogany table and "gothic" chairs to wine and dine friends and celebrities. Doubtless the drawing room, today furnished with japanned chairs and tortoiseshell writing cabinets, was also an informal place for the discussions to continue.

But among the celebrities were no ordinary men. Those who met regularly at his house whenever there was a full moon were men at the leading edge of research and inquiry. Without street lamps, nights when the moon was full were safest for travel. As a result, the conferees became known as the Lunar Society

To be sure, there were innocuous social gatherings aplenty but Boulton had been blessed with an inquiring mind and used these evenings around a wine bottle or two to explore the latest developments in science and technology.

MEETINGS OF GREAT MINDS

In the mid-18th century, British society was still very close to its rural routes. A maelstrom of advances were transforming it faster than at any other time in history. Yet knowledge was not so extensive that long training was required to understand any branch of it. Any educated and intelligent man could keep abreast of the progress. Indeed, progress was often made by relatively uneducated men who seemingly emerged from nowhere to become great factory masters and exceedingly wealthy.

There were many similar societies but none had such a distinguished membership as that which met at Soho House. Boulton was the prime mover but his fourteen guests included James Watt (steam), Erasmus Darwin (physician and grandfather of Charles Darwin), Josiah Wedgwood (pottery), James Kier (chemist and glass maker), Joseph Priestley (oxygen) and William Withering (digitalis), Dr. Thomas Day (anti-slavery campaigner and children's books) and R.L.Edgeworth,(inventor of mechanical devices).

Although the term lunar refers to the time of the month when members of the Society met, Boulton had his own observatory on the roof to further his interest in the Heavens.

The 18th century was a time not only of unparalleled openness but of enthusiastic questioning and inquiry. Men gathered frequently in informal groups to answer the question 'Why?" and "How" and to discuss and even demonstrate the latest experiments. Overseas, other men delved into the far corners of the world to explore, to discover new countries and peoples and to bring back unknown flora and fauna.

History was made when the Lunar Society met in this dining room

All this was discussed in the sumptuous surroundings of Soho House. Boulton, of course, was no mere rich dilettante. The reputation of his Soho Manufactury was known the length and breadth of the land and in other lands besides.

Boulton's father had been a manufactureer of what were known at the time as "toys" but which, in fact ,were a range of metal articles such as watch chains, snuff boxes, shoe buckles and buttons. Cruets, sugar bowls and tongs were made for the dining table, candelabras for walls and ceilings and there were picture frames, mirrors, thimbles and scissors for ladies' work-tables. One of the factors which made "toy" manufacture profitable was that in an age when transport was barely developed the items were small and light but valuable in proportion to their bulk and weight. In effect, Boulton took over the family business from his father.

Like his contemporary, Josiah Wedgwood, Matthew Boulton saw an ever advancing frontier of profit as the middle-class expanded. Some items were even made out of gold

Matthew Boulton, with Soho Works in the background, proudly holding examples of his "toys."

or silver and could be very expensive. Birmingham became a centre for jewellery making and today its Jewellery Quarter attracts buyers and tourists alike.

The area around Birmingham was blessed with iron ore which could be smelted using local fuels, the blades of edge tools could be ground on local sandstones and machinery could be turned by the water power of the streams which flowed down from the watershed on which Birmingham stands. Edge tools, nails and chains were for long the main products of an area which would eventually become Britain's second largest city.

Matthew Boulton was born in 1728 and entered the family business in 1745. He was handsome, strong, sociable and charming and very quick to recognize the importance and utility of other men's inventions. In short, he was an entrepreneur, a man who could use his capital and managerial expertise to put to work the inventions of others. Men like James

Watt, would probably not have succeeded with his steam engines had it not been for Boulton. Where Watt was self doubting, Boulton was bold and while Watt was poor, Boulton was a successful businessman. It would make an ideal combination.

Boulton married into the wealthy Robinson family of Lichfield and there is no doubt that, had he wished, Boulton could have set himself up as a country gentleman, maintaining a mansion, a library for cultivated pleasure and a stable of hunters for sport. But Boulton was fascinated by the discoveries of the age and preferred to see his money put to work in the true spirit of capitalism.

Many of the products Boulton manufactured were originally made at workshops scattered around the town rather than in any central location. Birmingham manufacturer, John Taylor, had already blazed a trail by bringing all the processes and workers together under one roof, eliminating much waste of time and money.

CONSTANTLY EXTENDED

Boulton decided to follow suit and invested in a factory on a piece of barren land at Handsworth Heath, beside Hockley Brook. The works was constantly extended until it employed upwards of 700 workmen with accommodation also provided.

Raw materials were stored on site, manufacture undertaken at one location and there was a warehouse to store the finished goods prior to shipment. There were drawing and design rooms where new work would be planned and even an advertising and marketing section - all very modern. Boulton added many new novelties to Birmingham's traditional lines and vowed to "work for all Europe in all things that they may have occasion for: gold, silver, copper, plated, gilt, pinchbeck, steel, platina, tortoiseshell or anything else that may become an article of general demand." The profits rolled in.

Hockley Brook was too thin a stream to keep the water wheels which turned Soho's machines operating in dry weather. Horse gins were also used. But steam promised to be the ultimate saviour. If a pumping engine could take the water up from the tail race back to the mill pond the water could be used continuously, irrespective of the season or the conditions.

Luck was ever on Boulton's side. James Watt had been financed by John Roebuck of Carron Ironworks fame in Scotland. When Roebuck went bankrupt his share in Watt's patent for the rotary motion engine was transferred to Boulton and the way was clear for him to invite Watt to Soho.

Much of the profit from "toys" was now spent on attempts to perfect Watt's rotary steam engine. Rotary motion made it possible to apply steam power to a huge range of industrial processes and was truly more revolutionary than almost any other aspect of the Industrial Revolution.

From the outset, Boulton realised the world-wide possibilities of the steam engine much more clearly that Roebuck and was able to achieve much higher standards of accuracy. He wrote to Watt: " It would not be worth my while to make for three counties only; but I find it well worth my while to make for all the world."

Soho Manufactury already employed many of the craftsmen Watt needed to make the valves and other delicate parts of the engine. Cylinders were made by the great Midlands ironmaster, John Wilkinson, an exact contemporary of Boulton.

Boulton vowed to make Watt's engines: "twenty percent cheaper than it would otherwise be executed and with as great a difference of accuracy as between the blacksmith and the mathematical instrument maker.

The same principles used in the manufacture of "toys" would now be applied to the production of steam engines. At first Boulton and Watt merely acted as consultants. But seeing the opportunities, they quickly went into the manufacture of steam engines. Initially, they bought in parts they required but, as soon as practicable, Boulton erected at Soho "all the conveniences necessary for the completion of the engines" and in 1795, Soho Foundry opened its doors for business.

Modern mass production in factory conditions had now been applied to steam and Boulton and Watt engines found an increasing queue of customers from mines, ironworks and from the new factories burgeoning around the country. Wilkinson installed one of the first of Watt's and Boulton's steam engines to blow his blast furnaces at Broseley, near Coalbrookdale. Between 1775 and 1800, it is fair to say that Boulton and Watt dominated the manufacture of steam engines in Britain and throughout the world.

As trade increased throughout the country, currency became very short because each coin had to be made by

The thatched hermitage where he went to contemplate alone can also be visited in the grounds.

hand. It could also be easily counterfeited. Mulling over this problem, Boulton manufactured a machine to make coins and began output at Soho Mint.

Metal goods and steam engines made Matthew Boulton the biggest iron manufacturer of his day and the instigator of a partnership with James Watt which would make

Soho's engines famous around the world and for generations to come.

Soho House today reflects the interests and the success of this outstanding entrepreneur. Here can be seen the room where he met the most important scientists, engineers and thinkers of his time, some of his original furniture and the study where he checked his balance sheets and drew up plans which would revolutionize the manufacture of "toys," steam engines and even the coins of the realm. Displays tell the story of this fascinating man and there is a chance to see some of the products of Boulton's nearby factory and Mint - buttons, buckles, ormolu clocks and vases, silver and Sheffield plate.

Bearing in mind Boulton's fascination with iron and steam it is hardly surprising that Soho House was built to include metal window frames and was one of the first in Britain to have its own central heating. A furnace was located in the cellar and visitors can find out how the warm air system worked.

SOHO HOUSE
Soho Avenue,
off Soho Road,
Handsworth,
Birmingham B18 5LB
Tel: 0121 554 9122
www.bmag.org.uk

Where Matthew Boulton and James Watt helped make Birmingham the heart of the Workshop of the World.

138

During the period of the Industrial Revolution, Birmingham and the surrounding region became the world's first manufacturing centre. The city already had a long tradition of manufacture dating back to the Middle Ages - particularly in the production of metal goods. However, it was during the late 18th century that changes took place that were to alter the course of history, both for the city, the region and the rest of the world.

Thinktank tells this story through three exhibitions that feature some of the original engines and machines that played a key role in this story.

Water had been used as a power source for centuries, but it had its limitations. As manufacturing in Birmingham grew, so did the demand for power. By the 18th century, there was an actual shortage of streams - in addition to seasonal variations in the water supply. The invention of the steam engine was to change all this. People would not have to rely on natural sources of power - they could create their own power, whenever and wherever they needed it - and on a huge scale.

CRUCIAL DEVELOPMENTS

It was in Birmingham that James Watt - in partnership with Matthew Boulton - exploited his crucial developments in the steam engine. The "Smethwick Engine" that he designed in 1779 is featured at Thinktank, and is now the oldest working steam engine in the world. It was built by the local canal company to raise water for the canal. Watt's key innovation was a separate cold condenser that made it twice as powerful as any engine before.

Boulton and Watt patented this invention and, with the foresight of its impact, set up a business to manufacture steam engines. As Boulton described to a visitor - "I sell, Sir, what all the world desires to have - POWER". Initially, the two men simply designed the engines and made some of the specialist parts. By

Parts of the Murray Engine (right) and Rolling Mill Engines (left).

1796, they had set up a foundry in Smethwick to produce complete steam engines which were sold all over the world. The large faceplate lathe used at this foundry can be seen at Thinktank, together with some of Boulton and Watt's more personal items. These include Watt's ingenious design of a toasting fork, and his copy press which they used to take copies of all their business records.

Dating from a few years later, visitors can also see the revolutionary Murray engine, designed by Matthew Murray in 1802 and now the third oldest working steam engine in the world. Its innovation was to replace the usual big horizontal beam with a compact system of gears making it ideal for smaller factories.

Even before the Industrial Revolution, Birmingham had become a recognized centre in the production of metal goods

- "toys and trinkets". At this stage most of the products would have been made by hand. One of the important developments affecting Birmingham, as elsewhere, was the introduction of machines - the mechanization of production so that a greater range of goods could be produced more quickly. Thinktank displays a 'timeline' of such machines from the late 18th to the early 20th century, many still in operation. This starts with the button shank making machine, an example of a very early automatic production machine - dating from the 1790s. It was used in Birmingham to produce the shanks that go on the back of the metal buttons, which many Birmingham firms made.

The button shank machine also represents another key development of the Industrial Revolution - the division of labour- breaking down production into single processes. With traditional methods of manufacture, even making a simple object like a button could be a slow process, and workers had to be skilled in a range of different techniques. With the division of labour, unskilled workers could produce objects more quickly. The Soho Manufactory in Birmingham was a good example of this, with up to 800 employees making many thousands of small products each day.

During the 19th century, Birmingham became known as the "City of a Thousand Trades." Thinktank conveys something of the volume and variety of local production with a kaleidoscopic display of products made in Birmingham and the region. These range from cheap, mass-produced metal goods to hand crafted silver jewellery made in the famous 'Jewellery Quarter'. Many of these products were exported and some even appeared to come from factories in other countries, in an attempt to satisfy patriotic foreigners. A good example of this is the pen nibs which were made cheaply in Birmingham and exported all over the world, with a direct impact on global literacy. On certain days there are demonstrations of silversmithing close to the recreated workshop of Bernard Cuzner, one of Birmingham's most famous silversmiths.

The story of local manufacture is brought up to date with robots from a local car factory. Contrary to popular

Thinktank's resident silversmith at work in the Making Things gallery.

perception, manufacture is still an important part of the regional economy.

As an international centre of manufacturing, goods had to be transported out of the city and raw materials had to be brought in. Birminham is landlocked, and in the early days this meant using packhorses and wagons on poorly constructed roads. In the 18th century, the growth of the canal network was crucial in expanding Birmingham's trade. On the day that the first Birmingham Canal opened, all of eight kilometres long, the price of coal on Birmingham streets was halved. During the 19th century rail took over for longer distance transport, but many canals were kept in operation because they could link the factories to railway interchange yards.

Thinktank's 'Move It' game explores what it was like to use this network of canals, railways and roads. It challenges visitors to move different products made in Birmingham to one of Britain's ports for export - and to do this as quickly and cost effectively as possible.

Around this game visitors can see some 'star' vehicles of road and rail, such as the City of Birmingham steam locomotive, and the last surviving Birmingham electric tram. And to bring the transport story up to date, Thinktank features a dramatic display of cars, motorbikes and cycles, mostly made in Birmingham and the region.

Through its displays, Thinktank aims to show how innovation and ingenuity made Birmingham and the region a centre of manufacturing during the Industrial Revolution and beyond.

Local children following an interactive trail around the galleries.

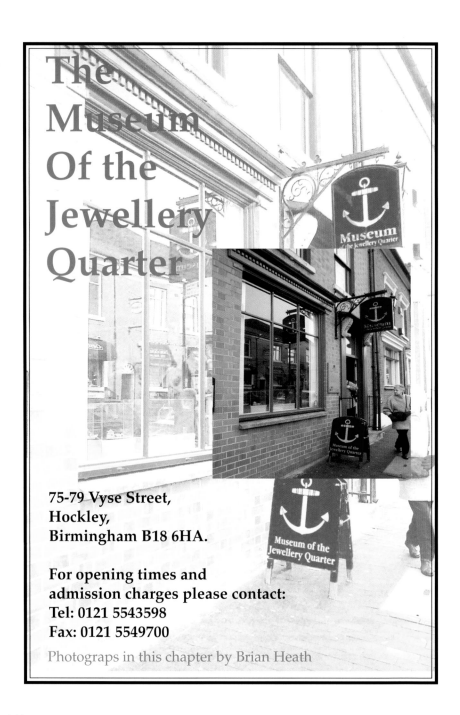

The Museum Of the Jewellery Quarter

75-79 Vyse Street,
Hockley,
Birmingham B18 6HA.

For opening times and
admission charges please contact:
Tel: 0121 5543598
Fax: 0121 5549700

Photograps in this chapter by Brian Heath

There was a time when Birmingham was the most famous manufacturing city in Britain, as well known in Bombay and Beijing as the world-class city of London.

Birmingham's reputation was based on the flood of small manufactured articles, often made of metal, which flowed out of the city's warrens of workshops.

Eighteenth century discoveries in metalworking were taken up faster in Birmingham than almost anywhere else, by the end of the century enabling it to revel in being known as the "toy shop of Europe" or the "Workshop of the World" - a title increasingly extended to Britain as a whole as the country soared above its rivals and competitors.

The ore from which iron was smelted to make Birmingham's metal trinkets, popularly known as 'toys,' was readily available nearby as was the coal needed for the generation of the steam which increasingly replaced human muscles in driving machines large and small. By the end of the 18th century the city was linked to the expanding canal system thus breaking out of its landlocked isolation.

But while it was factories of monstrous size eventually powered by huge steam engines which characterized the spinning industry further north, Birmingham's industrial evolution was based on a veritable army of small, family-size manufacturers, as often as not working from home and using an array of hand tools which owed little to steam.

As demand rose, workshops were thrown up in the gardens of craftsmen's houses where they soon turned out vast quantities of the 'toys' which home and even overseas markets could increasingly afford - buttons, buckles, boxes and other small ornamental metal goods in steel, brass and silver.

More than anything else Birmingham's growth owed itself to the fact that the Industrial Revolution expanded and even created domestic incomes while at the same time enabling the production of goods with enormous potential in export markets around the world.

A jeweller's bench and fly presses.

The so called small masters of Birmingham by no means dominated manufacture entirely. An outstanding exception was Matthew Boulton whose great Soho Works eventually employed 600 people making metal consumer items under large scale factory conditions. He also became well known for his partnership with James Watt, the two of them making Birmingham as famous for its steam engines as for its trinkets. Boulton's home, Soho House, is located close to the Jewellery Quarter and both can be visited within a day.

As the number of small masters increased, the downtown area of the city became cramped and a move began to more spacious surroundings in the north west around St. Paul's Square, on an estate known as New Hall which had once belonged to the Colmore family and which was eventually destined to become Birmingham's Jewellery Quarter. St. Paul's Church, built in 1776-79 for the local merchants, still stands and can be visited.

The demand for jewellery skyrocketed in the mid-19th century partly thanks to the discovery of gold in the United States and Australia and also to the availability of less expensive standards of gold alloy. Manufacture exploded. Many new manufacturers were lured into the jewellery trade and new workshops mushroomed.

The workshops were clustered together in the form visitors see in the Jewellery Quarter today. The putting out of work by factors or agents made it sensible to be close together and also the manufacture of individual items frequently involved the skills of multiple artisans and firms. From a production point of view it was an industry which lived off itself.

As had been the case in the making of metal goods at factories like Soho, after the mid-19th century purpose-built jewellery factories began to be built and some can still be seen today, often architecturally more grand and imposing than had been possible for craftsmen working from home.

Some of the more ramshackle of the Jewellery Quarter's myriad of works were demolished in the late 1960s and replaced by flatted factories, one of which, built in 1971 and known as the 'Big Peg,' continues in use today on the corner of Vyse Street.

Birmingham's Jewellery Quarter is both a unique flashback to the early day's of the city's industrial development and a living, evolving community of crafts people, manufacturers and retailers.

There are literally hours of fascination to be had either exploring the venerable buildings of the quarter or succumbing to the lure of the sparkle of precious stones, silver and gold which cram the shelves and display cabinets of retailers.

The Jewellery Quarter is Britain's biggest volume producer of gold jewellery and goods range from inexpensive nine carat gold earrings stamped out in thousands for the major high street multiples, to fine hand-made diamond jewellery, enamelling and silverware for leading London West End retailers

Mr Tom's office.

and for the palaces of the Middle East. To this day, Birmingham-made jewellery is still exported all over the world.

Like the Jewellery Quarter itself, the Museum of the Jewellery Quarter shows the visitor both past and present faces of a trade which once played a major part in the city's fortunes.

The Museum is built around the restored work-shops of an old Jewellery Quarter company, Smith & Pepper. Charles Smith and Edwin Pepper entered into partnership in 1899 occupying 77 and 78 Vyse Street and quickly building a workshop in the garden at the rear.

The partners made gold bangles, brooches, cufflinks, lockets and crosses and continued to make many of the same designs throughout their history, specializing in bracelets. They were particularly well known for "snake" bracelets and necklets and for "bamboo" bangles.

By 1914 the business was doing well enough to

replace the two old terrace houses with a new front office block, linked to the workshop in the back garden.

Three of Charles Smith's children continued the family business right up to 1981 when the company ceased trading locking up the workshops and offices exactly as they were on the last day of business. Birmingham City Council sensed that the old works could make a wonderful museum and stepped in to buy the premises before they became derelict..

With the addition of No 79 Vyse Street, it is this old Smith & Pepper factory which the modern visitor tours today, so painstakingly restored that those who once worked there say: "Yes, this is how it was. This is just how it was."

The Museum of the Jewellery Quarter tells the story of jewellery making in Birmingham, not just from the time of the Industrial Revolution, but from its true beginnings in Medieval times. You can explore this extraordinary industrial time capsule on a lively guided tour, finding things as they were in Smith & Pepper's heyday.

But the Museum of the Jewellery Quarter also tells a much bigger story than the history of Smith and Pepper. Here you can learn about the gold, silver, platinum, diamonds and coloured gemstones that are the jeweller's raw materials. Videos and displays show where and how they are mined and reveal some of the basic techniques of jewellery making.

The Museum shop sells original work by local designer jewellers as well as a wide variety of gifts and books. Refreshments are available in a light and airy cafe.

THE PEN ROOM

The Birmingham Pen Trade Heritage Association

Open: Mon-Sat: 11am-4pm. Sun: 1-4pm

Birmingham was the centre of the world pen trade for more than a century, employing thousands of people, mainly women, and pioneering craftsmanship, manufacturing processes and employment opportunities.

* See displays of hand presses and writing equipment

* Try writing with reed pens, quills, steel pens and typewriters or write Braille or moon

Find out how to write Chinese or other Asian scripts

*Learn about the history of the pen companies

Unit 3, The Argent Centre, 60, Frederick Street, Hockley, Birmingham B1 3HS. Tel: 0121 236 9834. Email: brianjones@pentalk.freeserve.co.uk. Web site: www.bptha.xoasis.com

Above: Forge Mill Needle Museum

Redditch and the areas around it were once not only the needle manufacturing capital of Britain but of the world.
The specialization in needle making developed slowly but, like many other areas of Britain during the Industrial Revolution, Redditch seems to have found that the road to survival lay in allowing itself to be caught up in a kind of national division of labour in which whole districts came to be dominated by a single industry.

The Forge Mill at Redditch, now the Forge Mill Needle Museum, began its life as an iron forge at the turn of the 18th century. An adjacent but abandoned site once occupied by Cistercian monks had a long history of metal working using water power.

A shortage of timber and the charcoal needed to smelt iron had encouraged ironmakers to migrate away from their traditional home in southeastern England to other parts of Britain where forests were still plentiful, such as areas close to the busy River Severn, including the Forest of Dean. Once iron had been cast, forges were needed to craft the myriad items of common use. But the forges needed water to drive giant water wheels which in turn powered the forge's heavy hammers. The site of Forge Mill Museum was a perfect location because it was in the Arrow Valley close to the River Arrow and a stream known locally as Red Ditch.

After Abraham Derby discovered how to smelt iron using coke at his furnaces at Coalbrookdale, Shropshire, the list of items made from iron increased exponentially but furnaces and forges tended to be set up close to coal fields and production took place in ever larger units.

Iron and coal were plentifully and easily available in north-east Worcestershire and South Staffordshire and this district along the river valleys of the Tame and Stour became Britain's largest single production area for metal items. Birmingham, just north of Redditch, was to become world famous for making a range of iron and metal items that it is often described as the very heart of the Workshop of the World.

The owners of Forge Mill faced a time of unprecedented opportunity but also of stiff competition. Should they continue to satisfy local demand for such things as stirrups, horseshoes, carriage and cart parts and locks or should they look for something different in which to specialise and which could command a larger market?

Just as corn mills were frequently converted to iron slitting, by 1739, when the first needle maker is recorded at the village of Studley, Redditch Forge Mill had been converted from iron making to needle scouring or polishing.

For centuries needles had been made by blacksmiths from sheet iron to satisfy local demand. However, the Tudor kings and queens encouraged specialised needle makers from Germany and the Low Countries to settle in London. Gradually, other needle making centres were established at Chichester and Long Crendon in Buckinghamshire

Manniquins show off aspects of needle making and emphasise that many of the workers were women and children

as well as in the Arrow Valley. Once established at Studley, needle making spread to villages within a radius of 10 miles and soon developed into an extensive cottage industry in the area.

Within a century, Redditch had become the major centre for needle making throughout Britain. Machines were introduced to increase the rate of production and work which used to be done in cottages was now brought under one roof with all the benefits of regular time keeping and division of labour.

Forge Mill reached its heyday during the Victorian period when many of the improvements to the techniques of needle making emanated from Redditch. By 1870, the Redditch needle making district was manufacturing 3,500 million needles of all types per year. So great was its contribution that rival centres of needle making went into decline.

Needles, one might think, don't seem to have much use other than for stitching on loose buttons but that was far from the case when most clothes were hand-made. Even when sewing machines were invented needles were still required. The population virtually doubled in the 18th century creating the kind of demand which encouraged the invention of the factory system as a means of keeping up with it. People needed clothes and the textile and garment trades quickly became the largest employers in the country - with a concomitant need of needles. Wherever clothes were being made, needles were required, not to mention also by shoe makers and glove makers. Even sail makers and the jute bag makers of Dundee used needles. There were needles of many thicknesses and lengths serving many purposes.

And then, of course, needles were needed for fish hooks - in effect a curved needle with a barb. By the turn of the 20th century Redditch became the home of Allcocks, the largest manufacturer of fishing tackle in the world.

Steel had been used to make needles since it was first invented and in making needles the people of Redditch had perfected their skills in working spring steel enabling them to make springs for just about everything from beds through vehicles to anglepoise lamps.

After Forge Mill started to provide needle scouring services it became a magnet for needle makers. When water power was used to scour and point needles the result was a higher quality and relatively cheap needle. The Mill owners and Redditch has discovered their comparative advantage. And like Birmingham with its "toys," Redditch had hit upon manufacturing articles which were inexpensive to transport at a time when the cost of moving heavy or bulky items by road remained high.

The East Wing of Forge Mill Needle Museum dates to 1828 and today visitors can find out about the fascinating and sometimes gruesome story of needle making in Redditch. By means of displays and recreated scenes, visitors see how the coils of steel wire which arrived from the Black Country or Sheffield were drawn down to the required thickness. The atmosphere is often dark and gloomy and keep in mind that in the 18th and early 19th centuries the work was carried out by candlelight. Next they see how the wire was cut into appropriate lengths to make needles and how the needles were pointed - once the most dangerous job in needle manufacture because of the danger of flying slivers of metal and the unhealthy inhalation of dust given off by the pointer's stone. The needle eyes were formed by men and women using stamping and eyeing machines, the men stamping and the women eyeing. Women and even children worked removing excess metal from around the eye in a process known as spitting. Once formed, the needles were too soft to use until hardened in the furnace. Needles bent in the process were straightened out by women using small hammers and anvils. An exciting audio tour brings all of the machinery and processes vividly to life. Occasionally there are characters in costume and role playing for school children.

Between the East and West Wings you will see the water wheel which powers the scouring beds and associated machinery. The scouring mill itself remains much as it was in 1958 when last used and the tools and materials used in the scouring process can still be seen. The needles were scoured 60,000 at a time in wooden troughs or setts using soft soap, grease and emery powder. After scouring the needles were glazed using a mixture of olive oil and oxide of tin. Inside the West Wing is the Barrelling Shop where the needles were dried and just outside the Stone Crushing Shed where old pointing stones were crushed into scouring powder.

If you return to the East Wing, the top floor shows the many types and uses of needles. Uses range from beading to bookbinding and sail making to smocking. There are also examples of some of the old crafts and pasttimes using specialist needles, like tambour work, embroidery, tapestry and leather work. The displays include the world's largest and smallest needles.

During a period when Britain has given up many of the industries which made it famous, needles are still produced in the Redditch area today. The Museum's collection is brought up to date with a Redditch surgical needle, used to stitch some of the barrier tiles onto the space shuttle Columbia.

Forge Mill Museum is a regional centre for textile enthusiasts and mounts textile exhibitions each year.

To the north of Forge Mill can be found Bordesley Abbey, founded by Cistercian monks in 1138. The Cistercians sought isolation to practice their beliefs. The monks diverted the River Arrow to improve the drainage of the site and to supply water to to an artificial mill pond which provided the water to drive an undershot wheel which powered trip hammers and bellows in connection with metal and leather working. Today, little of the Abbey is visible above ground but the site is one of the most important monastic precincts in Europe. Bordesley Abbey Visitor Centre tells the Abbey's story and displays finds from 25 years of archaeological exploration.

Below right: A display of Redditch fish hooks.

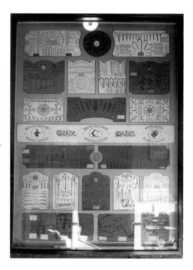

For opening times and admission charges pleasecontact:

**Tel: 01527 62509
Email:
museum@redditchbc.gov.uk.**

**Needle Mill Lane,
Riverside,
Redditch,
Worcestershire B98 8HY**

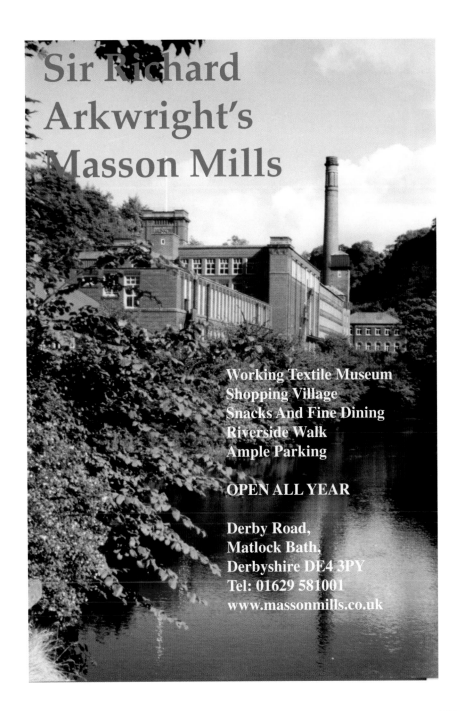

Sir Richard Arkwright's Masson Mills

Working Textile Museum
Shopping Village
Snacks And Fine Dining
Riverside Walk
Ample Parking

OPEN ALL YEAR

Derby Road,
Matlock Bath,
Derbyshire DE4 3PY
Tel: 01629 581001
www.massonmills.co.uk

Way In - welcome to the Textile Museum

F ew users of the A6 between Matlock and Derby can fail to notice the huge sign on the facade of Masson Mill at Matlock Bath: "Sir Richard Arkwright & Co. Established 1769."

But only those in the know probably realise that the four-storey mill once belonged to the man who has become known as the "Father Of The Factory System."

Like other mills out of sight or scattered throughout Derbyshire, Yorkshire and Lancashire, the immense barrack-like structures at the northern gateway to the Derwent Valley World Heritage Site now seem locked forever in the time of "dark Satanic mills."

Yet the reality was that when such mills were first built more than 250 years ago, usually in remote locations close to fast flowing rivers, the glow of lamps at night from their many storeys was as brilliant as the lights of Manhattan today. Machinery hummed night and day in an atmosphere reminiscent of Silicon Valley's computer boom of the 1980s.

It was by no means all sweetness and light. Cottage workers whose jobs were threatened by new machines sometimes smashed the threats to their livelihoods and even threatened the lives of their inventors. When he became the wealthiest mill owner in the land some of Arkwright's factories were burnt to the ground by workers who preferred the old ways. At Cromford and Matlock Bath, Arkwright could call on 600 men, 1,000 guns and even canon, should the need have arisen.

The world's largest collection of bobbins

Between 1750 and 1801 in Britain, the population virtually doubled. Wherever there were young adults there were young children and not just one or two but droves of them. Overseas, Britain's foreign trade was expanding throughout the Americas, the Caribbean and Africa, India, China and the Far East. Great sailing ships brought raw materials into the country and shipped finished goods out. Demand for consumer goods by people at home and customers abroad was insatiable.

The watchword of the

One of the original boilers used to power the mighty steam engine which kept Masson Mills' machines clattering day and night.

time was "production." Produce, produce and produce again. For any man of an entrepreneurial bent there were riches to be made from manufacture - if only technical constraints could be overcome and men with the right mindset could be found. Just such a man was Richard Arkwright.

He was born in Preston, Lancashire, in 1732, one of thirteen children in a poor working family. While he learned to read and write, as a child, the potential benefits of these skills were lost on him and, as soon as he could, he abandoned his books and went to work in a barber's shop as a lather boy, soon quitting to work for a wig maker in Bolton.

While he may not have been an ardent student, Arkwright was an enthusiastic worker who knew the value of hard work and of money. When his employer died and while he himself was hardly more than 20 years of age Arkwright was able to carry on the business by himself, an experience which doubtless led him to set up on his own as soon as he could. Typical of the man, his shop offered BOTH barbering and wig making and on the strength of his success at the age of 23 he married his first wife, Patience Holt.

ENDLESS POSSIBILITIES

Arkwright was clearly a bright lad. He discovered a waterproof dye for his wigs when nobody else could find it and loved to tinker and improve any mechanical devices in his shop. Around him the world was being shaken by the beginnings of the industrial revolution. Inventions flowed thick and fast, news of them carried far and wide thanks to a road building mania which increased the number of travellers to record numbers. On every side men were talking about old things being done in new ways and even about new things unimaginable only a short time before. The possibilities for enrichment were unique and endless. What a time to live!

When Arkwright's first wife died after child birth he married again in 1761 to Margaret Biggins, a lady with money. The couple bought a bigger and better shop at a more attractive

Visitors can see spinning machines in action at the Working Museum

location and the business continued to expand. Lucrative wig making for the fashionable took preference over barbering and Arkwright spent much of his time travelling on horseback by turnpike or forest track scouring the country for girl's hair for his wigs.

A traveller, of course, meets many people and hears many things. Around the workmen's cottages, especially the weavers with their many daughters with full heads of hair, Arkwright could not have failed to come to know about the crisis in spinning.

The demand for garments was booming at home and abroad but weavers were being held back by the fact that the output of a single spinning wheel was limited. Even the hands of a whole family spinning could not keep a weaver fully supplied. On average, it required four spinners to support one weaver. To make matters worse, the invention by John Kay in 1733 of the flying shuttle had quickened the speed of weaving! Other improvements to the loom widened the cloth further increasing the pressure on spinners. James Hargreaves' spinning jenny ameliorated the difficulty by carrying several spindles but it was still limited in output by its size and by virtue of being manually operated. Whoever could even more dramatically increase the output of yarn stood to be rich indeed! The Society of Arts was even offering prizes for whoever invented improved spinning machines which actually worked!

Recognising the possibilities thrown up by the shortage of yarn, Arkwright worked on the solution to the extent of giving up his business. He had his own ideas but he benefited from close collaboration with Warrington clock maker, John Kay, whom he met in 1767. Neither were free of competition. Others also saw the possibilities.

COMPLETE MECHANISATION

Lewis Paul had patented a roller spinning machine as early as 1738 with power supplied by donkeys. When the experiment failed Edward Cave bought the patent and tried his own hand. Ultimately the patent fell into the hands of Richard Arkwright who succeeded in correcting the defects of Paul's machine and patented his own now famous water frame in 1769. Within a decade he patented ten other inventions, including the carding machine and the roving frame, thus completing the mechanisation of the preparatory processes of the cotton trade and leaving only weaving to the hand industry.

Arkwright's water frame passed a strand of cotton thread through a roller where it was compressed and sent on to a second set of rollers. These were turning at a faster speed than the first set thus lengthening the strand. From these rollers the cotton passed on to a revolving spindle which gave the twist to the yarn, before being wound round a bobbin.

Scholars generally agree that Arkwright's claims to be the inventor of the water frame, hotly contested at the time, rest on doubtful ground. But like many another capitalists of the

It was the constant and plentiful water supply of the River Derwent that led Arkwright to build Masson Mill, his greatest mill, on the banks of the river at Matlock Bath

time his true genius lay not so much in the water frame but in mobilising and controlling the capital which made large scale use of his machine feasible and, in turn, in putting the machines efficiently to work in a factory environment so as to achieve the prodigious output the market craved, hence his name the Father of the Factory System

           In the early years, Arkwright was perpetually short of money and his difficulties were only solved once he entered into partnership with Samuel Need of Nottingham and Jedediah Strutt of Derby, both engaged in the Nottingham hosiery trade. Arkwright originally envisaged that the water frame would be worked by horse power and his first mill, built in

Nottingham, was little more than a workshop with a few frames powered by horse gins.

But Arkwright was desperate to take advantage of the possibilities offered by the times and expand output. By 1771, after he had joined forces with Need and Strutt, he had the capital to build a much bigger factory at Cromford, Derbyshire, modelled on the silk mill first established by Thomas Cotchett at Derby in 1718 and in 1721 taken over by John Lombe - a mill powered not by horses but by fast flowing water and generally recognised as Britain's very first true factory. Significantly, when it went into use in 1771, Arkwright's spinning machine was known as the "water frame."

Today, Derby Industrial Museum occupies the site of Lombs's mill at the southern end of the World Heritage Corridor. Strutt built his own mills and workers' cottages at Belper and Millford, parts of which can still be seen as a component of the World Heritage Site. In fact, the Site includes an incredible 867 listed buildings.

EXCEPTIONAL FORCE

Arkwright was frequently in the Cromford area and would have known that the Derwent was a fast flowing river of exceptional force which never froze - Masson Mill still supplies the National Grid with electricity. Cromford and Matlock Bath were ideal locations, fast flowing water, plentiful labour, close to the Nottingham hosiery trades and centrally placed between Liverpool, Hull and London, the ports receiving raw cotton. At first goods were shipped in and out by pack horse; then by canal.

Most males in the area worked in local lead mines which meant that Arkwright had a good supply of female and child labour. He was known as a fair if not benevolent employer, insisting on an order and cleanliness unknown in the rural hamlets from which his workers hailed. He employed no children below the age of ten years and they must have learnt to read and write before entering his service. Although his mills worked 24 hours a day he was no tyrant and even paid overtime. He

Visitors can purchase cloth woven in the Museum - for £1 per yard.

established a market and fair at nearby Cromford and held an annual workers festival at his mills known as "candle-lighting" at which there would be a parade with musical bands and free buns, fruit, nuts and ale.

Arkwright treated his workers well, building cottages for his weavers at Cromford and adding a school, a chapel and an inn where he could meet customers and guests, the Greyhound Hotel, all of which is within walking distance of Masson Mill. The weavers' cottages he built can still be seen at North Street, Cromford and at other locations round about. Arkwright built several more mills in the Derbyshire area and Masson, the greatest of them, was constructed in 1784. The mill has been extensively enlarged but Arkwright's original building can still be easily identified.

Masson Mills were the oldest mills in the world in continuous production until 1991. Families whose members have worked at Masson Mills for generations are still represented on

Food and drink aplenty at the Derwent Restaurant

the workforce, continuing the unbroken thread of employment back to 1784. It is said that Sir Richard's ghost treads the floor boards of the old mill.

Like any true capitalist, Arkwright was driven by the desire to acquire money and the excitement of getting it. He became the richest commoner in Britain with a personal fortune of over £500,000 and cherished the ambition of amassing enough money to pay off the National Debt. Arkwright was knighted in 1786 and appointed Sheriff of Derbyshire the following year.

He did not stint expense on himself and his family, driving out in a glittering coach with richly attired attendants. Until 1788, he lived in a house near to the mills but subsequently purchased a large estate owned by the father of Florence Nightingale, overlooking Masson Mills, where he resolved to build himself a castle. Willersley Castle is still there today and provides accommodation to visitors. But Arkwright never lived in it, dying before the castle could be completed following a fire during construction.

Masson Mills Working Textile Museum houses a unique and comprehensive collection of authentic working textile machinery which brings Arkwright's world alive to the visitor. You can watch cloth being woven and there is a good range available for purchase at £1 per yard. In the spinning and doubling room and the weaving shed spinners and weavers daily show the complex ways in which our clothes were once made, some of the clattering machines driven by overhead line-shafting and leather belting drives which are a fascination in themselves. Future plans at the heritage site include the restoration of steam power to the belting. The bobbin room contains nearly 700,000 different bobbins and is the largest collection in the world.

Because of the interest of the Mills and its museum, the Derwent Restaurant was early-on factored into the attractions providing food and drink far beyond mere "tea." Today, the smart 120-seat restaurant provides fine meals at reasonable prices. And for those whose tour has turned their thought to garments, there are four floors of quality shopping with high street names and specialty goods. Visitors can find not only an Aladdin's Cave of clothes of all shapes, colours and sizes but gifts, golfing accessories, perfumes and soaps, traditional and local foods, dried fruits, nuts and confectionery. A large car park makes visiting hassle free.

Bargains galore in the four floors of retail outlets at Masson Mills' Shopping Village

167

Sir Richard Arkwright's
Cromford Mills

Mill Lane,
Cromford, Derbyshire.
Tel and Fax: 01629 823256
Email: info@arkwrightsociety.org.uk
www.arkwrightsociety.org.uk

Please call for opening times and admission charges

Richard Arkwright is often described as the 'Father of the Factory System' in Britain and it is remarkable that more than 200 years after it was built we can still visit his spinning mills at Cromford, Derbyshire. Cotton spinning quit Derbyshire for Lancashire in the 19th century and from the second half of the 19th century, the old mills were put to other industrial uses until they were fortunately acquired for posterity by the Arkwright Society in 1979.

When they were built, the great, barrack-like mill buildings were regarded as a wonder of the age. They towered over the little cottages of the countryfolk and at night, with lights streaming from their hundreds of windows, the mills must have looked something like a land-bound 'Titanic.'

Arkwright's was not the first mill in the Derwent Valley. In 1721, John Lombe built a silk mill at Derby where the city's industrial museum now stands on its foundation arches. Like Arkwright's first mill it had five storeys and was driven by a water wheel. The mill gave local people a first taste of factory conditions and about 200 worked there.

To this day, no one knows how Arkwright came to invent a spinning machine which became one of the foundation blocks of the Industrial Revolution but he was undoubtedly what we might term a canny fellow.

Born in Preston he was the son of a tailor and therefore immersed in the world of garments and textiles at a time when it was more common than today for sons to follow fathers into the family business. It is hard to imagine that he did not overhear his father talking about how much more could be made or how costs might be reduced if only some way could be found to increase the output of Britain's thousands of cotton spinners working in cottages up and down the land - often alongside husbands who with the rest of the family operated hand looms.

Population was rising, trade was increasing, and weaving had already been improved by the invention of the flying shuttle. The bottleneck was spinning. If fibres could be

An aerial view of Cromford Mills

spun more quickly more could be woven and the supply of textiles increased.

At first, Arkwright turned his back on all this and like many a young man went off in a direction of his own. He worked as a barber and soon travelled around the country making and selling wigs.

With opportunities for profit accumulating unrequited around him, Arkwright's attention was drawn back to spinning through his association with one Thomas Highs of Leigh. Highs gave Arkwright the opportunity to work with him in experimenting to find ways of spinning more yarn. Some progress had already been made in the mid-1760s by James Hargreaves' invention of the spinning jenny by means of which a woman could spin multiple threads at the same time. But the device was primarily of benefit to cottage and workshop production and left production far short of what men like Arkwright assessed as the market's potential. Highs and Arkwright were assisted by Lancashire clock maker John Kay and in 1768 he and Kay perfected a roller spinning machine which came to be known as the spinning frame and later, the waterframe, because it was powered by water. Unlike the spinning jenny, the waterframe was simple to use even by young people with very little training. It was the simplicity as well as the capability of the waterframe that made large scale production possible and ushered in the factory system.

At first Arkwright lacked even the money to register his patent but in 1769 he successfully found two local men willing to invest. Patent in hand, he moved to Nottingham where he rightly assessed that demand would be higher for the relatively coarse but comparatively cheaper yarn his frame produced. He and Kay were able to establish a few frames in a horse powered workshop with the help of two merchant employers in the hosiery trade, Samuel Need and Jedediah Strutt.

But what were a few frames operated by a horse gin compared to market demand and the possibilities for profit? If many frames could be put to use output would sky rocket. Power was the limiting factor. The rotary steam engine had not yet been invented and was not applied in textile mills until 1785. Apart from horses the only other power available to Arkwright was that of water.

In August, 1771, he began to build a water powered five-storey mill on the fast flowing Bonsall Brook at Cromford. The Brook's flow was increased by its union with the Cromford Sough, a lead mine drain. The enthusiasm of the partners can be gauged from the fact that the shell of the first mill was practically complete by December 1771. One can imagine that the atmosphere was feverish and that the quiet countryside around Cromford had suddenly been transformed into something like the proverbial boom town of the American West.

Business was so good that in 1776 Arkwright built a second and very much larger mill at Cromford. Subsequently in 1785-86 the first mill building was extended and a new mill/ warehouse erected close to the access road from Cromford. The Bonsall Brook and Cromford Sough were separated. Water from the Sough was delivered to the mills via a raised embankment and aqueduct, making it possible to install a larger wheel. In later years, as more mills were built and as they grew in size, it became necessary to increase the water supply and improve the efficiency of the waterwheels and a series of reservoirs were constructed along the course of the Bonsall Brook of which the Greyhound Pond was the lowest.

There's always time for a break at Cromford Mills' cosy cafe.

In 1771, advertisements were placed in local newspapers urgently seeking craftsmen as well as the women and children who would operate the waterframes. It was not so easy to find the workers he needed at Cromford but by luring them from outside Arkwright took on the responsibility of housing them and so the growth of Cromford community began. Rows of cottages were built, the earliest in North Street, many of which can still be seen. These had three storeys and on the top floor weaving looms were set up making the yarn from the new mills into fabric.

There was also the Black Greyhound Inn, now the Greyhound Hotel, a chapel and a Saturday market at which, to encourage trade, Arkwright awarded prizes to the traders who sold the most goods. Once a year Arkwright held a festival for his workpeople. In 1776, to celebrate the completion of his second mill, about 500 workpeople and children, led by a band, paraded round the village watched by a large crowd. On their return to the mill they were suitably regaled with ale and buns and a ball followed in the evening. Arkwright's skill in managing a workforce which had never worked in factories before and at a time when many looked down on the work was as much a part of his genius as his technical expertise and financial acumen.

Visitors to this historic site today are immediately immersed in the atmosphere of the late 18th century - massive stone buildings, long lines of identical windows, narrow doorways, wooden beams, many still with the dark stains of smoke from oil lamps and uneven floors. Only the heat, the machines and their deafening clatter and the largely women and children who tended them are missing. But even these missing elements are brought back to life at an evocative exhibition of photographs on display in the annexe to the second mill, close to the main entrance. The building was once linked to a second mill at first floor level. Here, faces from the past gaze out at us as we try to imagine lives lived in 12 hour shifts which enabled the mills to operate day and night.

After the success of his first mill, Arkwright spent some time perfecting his machinery and mechanising many of the other parts of the spinning process, such as the carding and cleaning of the cotton. The second mill at the Cromford site, 129 feet long and seven storeys high and therefore considerably larger than the first mill reflects the success of his attempts to mechanise the whole spinning process. Unfortunately, this building was destroyed by fire in 1890 but excavations have revealed the ground plan of the mill and its great wheel pit.

Other large and spacious buildings still to be seen at the site were used either as warehouses or for the unmechanised processes associated with spinning. Some were doubtless used as workshops where machinery used at the mills were built and maintained. Today, the buildings have been restored. Some are in use as offices and on the ground floor a number of units have been converted into shops, including the mill shop selling an extremely wide range of Industrial Revolution literature as well as guidebooks to the site and gifts.

Arkwright established the pattern of early mill building; the plain, long, thin rectangular design thirty feet wide is characteristic of the early cotton mills. Lavatory columns, stair wells and offices were attached to the main building in such a way as not to detract from the factory floor space. Evidence of this can be seen at the main gates where the buildings are essentially rectangular with semi-circular extensions keyed in at the top, housing the stair well and offices.

Such is the seminal importance of Arkwright's buildings to the development of the factory system which changed the lives of millions of people around the world that Cromford now has the distinction of being part of the Derwent Valley Mills World Heritage Site.

At the western end of the Cromford site lies Grace Cottage which is thought to have been a gate keeper's house and which was built as one of a pair with the red brick building next to it. . The five-storey stone building behind it was a weavers' workshop where yarn spun in the mills was woven into cloth. The mill manger's house stands across the road opposite the mill entrance. Rock House, where Sir Richard Arkwright lived, stands on the hill overlooking the site, giving him an excellent view of those who worked for him. Arkwright built himself a grand new house, Willersely Castle, which overlooks Cromford from the north. Building began in 1788 but the unfinished interior was gutted by fire in 1791 and the house was still not complete when Sir Richard died a year later, the first and wealthiest capitalist of Britain. Today, Willersley Castle is a hotel but it serves as a conspicuous reminder of the wealth, power, position and taste that Arkwright acquired during his twenty revolutionary years at Cromford.

Richard Arkwright lies in a bricked-up vault inside St. Mary's Church, originally intended as a private chapel and mausoleum for the Arkwright family but opened to public

Cromford Mills Annexe is home to a picture and photo display which

worship by Richard Arkwright Junior in 1797. The church is a short walk from the mill, en route to the Cromford Canal and Wharf.

There are no noisy barges at the Wharf hauling in and out the materials Arkwright needed or made at his mill and the tranquil and beautiful surroundings make it an ideal spot for a picnic or a base for the start of a pleasant walk. In fact, the Arkwright Society has devised a local history trail only two miles in length but which includes all the major Cromford sites.

Hodgkinson's Hotel

150, South Parade,
Matlock Bath,
DE4 3NR
Tel: 01629 582170
Fax: 01629 584891

Email:
enquiries@hodgkinsons-hotel.co.uk
www.hodgkinsons-hotel.co.uk
Character, comfort and cuisine are the
hallmarks of this Grade II listed hotel,
centrally located at Matlock Bath. Now
fully restored to reflect its Victorian past,
with seven individually designed and
decorated en-suite rooms. Sample the best
of local peak produce imaginatively
prepared by Hodgkinson's Italian chef
proprietor.

Willersley Castle

Cromford, Matlock,
Derbyshire DE4 5JH
Tel: 01629 582270. Fax: 01629 582329
Email: cghwillers@aol.com
Built for Sir Richard Arkwright, Willersley
Castle offers the thrill of staying in an 18th
century factory master's house. Spectacu-
lar park land location overlooking the River
Derwent belies extremely reasonable
prices. Longe, TV & music rooms, meals
& refreshments. Gifts.

Sheriff Lodge

www.**Sheriff Lodge**.co.uk

Matlock - in the Heart of the
Derbyshire Dales.
Luxury, and so much more than a
Bed & Breakfast.
Tel: 01629 760760
Fax: 01629 760860
Email: info@sherifflodge.co.uk

Riverbank House

Derwent Avenue,
Off Olde
English Road,
Matlock DE4 3LX.
Tel: 01629 582593
Fax: 01629 580885

Email: bookings@riverbankhouse.co.uk
www.riverbankhouse.co.uk
Riverbank House, beautiful Victorian home
on the banks of the River Derwent. A
tranquil spot only minutes from all
amenities. Relax and enjoy a warm
welcome from the Newberry family.
Fishing rights, garden, log fires and
parking. Featured on Peak Practice.
Special offer - mid-week four nights for
three. German spoken. B&B from £24
pppn.

Wortley Top Forge

The Top Forge

Wortley Top Forge dates from the 1620s and is not only Wortley's but the world's oldest surviving heavy iron forge. Hidden away amid rolling hills in a wooded river valley just south of Barnsley, the Forge is a unique and irreplaceable fragment of Britain's early industrial history.

In both the building which houses the forge and in its products we can trace important stages of the unfolding of the Industrial Revolution.

Prior to 1709, when Abraham Darby succeeded in smelting cast iron with coke at Coalbrookdale, Shropshire, cast iron had traditionally been smelted using charcoal and wrought iron had been worked with the aid of water powered forge hammers.

While the Sussex iron industry was dying for lack of charcoal, the Don Valley remained heavily wooded and the

River Don provided an all year round source of power either for blast furnace bellows or forge hammers.

It was sometime between 1602 and 1625 that local landowner, Sir Francis Wortley, decided to capitalize on his increasingly valuable assets by establishing a forge to make malleable wrought iron. In fact, he built two, Top Forge and another further down the river known appropriately enough as Lower Forge, now derelict.

It was a brave initiative because there was very little iron working in Yorkshire at that time although there is evidence of Cistercian monks forging iron four hundred years earlier. Sir Francis not only grew the trees needed to make charcoal but could obtain furnace sandstone from local quarries and pig iron from furnaces located nearby. His gamble paid off and by the end of the 17th century Wortley Top was one of a cluster of successful blast furnaces and forges in South Yorkshire.

The building that visitors see today does not date from Sir Francis's time but from the 18th century. Extensive alterations were made to the building to accommodate new developments in iron making, especially Henry Cort's discovery in 1784 of a puddling and rolling process which enabled coal to be used to refine pig iron into malleable bar iron. A reverberatory puddling furnace was erected at Wortley Top Forge in 1787 together with a bar rolling mill, the first with grooved rolls to be installed in Yorkshire. Today, visitors can see an old mill of similar type rescued from Low Forge.

After 1774, steam began to be used to power both blast furnaces and forge hammers, for example, at Blaenavon, in South Wales, now a World Heritage Site. While keeping up with changes in iron making technology, the Wortley forges never abandoned water power to drive their heavy hammers and the water wheels can still be seen at the works today. Incredibly, they were still in use until World War 1 and after when in 1912 Top Forge closed with Low Forge ceasing wrought iron production in 1929.

In the early part of the 19th century railways so revolutionized transport as to create an explosion of demand for many kinds of items made of iron, including iron axles for the new locomotives and rolling stock. Railway mania got under way in earnest after 1830 and the owners of Wortley Top were quick to try to cash in. From the middle of the decade onwards, Wortley Top specialized in the production of high quality railway axles with the proud boast that a Wortley Top-made axle would never fail. It also specialized in the production of high quality bar-iron. The Forge thus became a pioneering example of integrated engineering, combining research, design, manufacture and testing.

The forge we see today is an axle forge which drew its supplies of wrought iron billet from Low Forge. The building is mainly 18th century and the forges date from the axle production of the 19th century.

When the visitor first enters the Forge it seems cavernous and dark. When the "Jack Roof' or raised roof is opened, light floods in. The original purpose was to allow more

The No. 1 hammer and water wheel

ventilation in an area containing furnaces capable of reaching temperatures in excess of 1300 degrees centigrade.

Axles were made from bundles of square bars up to two inches square built up into "faggots" of 16 bars held together with an iron hoop, the longer bars in the middle protruding at each end. Huge wooden cranes with iron working parts were used to enable the "faggot" to be placed in the furnace and brought to white heat before being swung through an arc to be pounded with one of the great hammers into the proper shape for an axle. One axle on display at the Forge weighs 300 LB. The cast iron hammer heads, attached to a wooden beam, are of a type used in Britain since the 16th century and can deliver blows to the anvil with a force of up to three tons. The furnaces, examples of which can still be seen, would have been iron boxes fitted with counter-balanced lift up doors.

The work of the forge men was dirty, noisy and dangerous. Slaggy matter might fly off from the hammers and cause serious injuries. To protect themselves the men wore face masks of wire mesh and were covered from neck to ankle by leather aprons. To protect their legs and feet they wore boots with iron feet and shin guards which almost reached up to their knees. The heat and glare was blinding, the noise of hammers beating at more than a hundred times a minute was deafening. The men worked in these conditions for eleven hours at a time.

The great waterwheels which powered the forge hammers and the adjacent blast furnace can still be seen and still turn.

Wheel No 1 is a superb example of a cast iron wheel which originally would have rotated around a wooden shaft. Before the advances in iron making the entire wheel would have been made of wood and around the Forge are numerous other examples of the transition from wooden wheels through iron hooped wooden wheels to wheels made entirely of iron. You can almost feel the industrial revolution unfolding before your eyes.

The cast iron Blower Wheel used in the blast furnace has a gear along one edge which was used to drive a shaft connected by belt-drive to various machines, including, at various times, an axle testing machine and an electric generator.

Keeping the Forge in operation required the back-up services of blacksmith, wheel right and joiner and the buildings that housed these services are used today to exhibit various aspects of work and life during the time of the Forge.

To the right of the main entrance is an area devoted to the crafts and skills of the blacksmith but the remainder has been given over to the reconstruction of a 19th century machine shop. The various lathes, drilling and shaping machines are driven by overhead line shafting in true steam-era fashion although today they are driven by paraffin engines. Many of the engines on display reflect advances in engine technology. Upstairs, is a changing exhibition of gas and electric appliances and hand tools of yesteryear.

Adjoining the Forge are two workers cottages and one has been furnished with the household items and curios typical of the time when workmen often lived on site. Around the Forge yard are many examples of the axles and wheels for which it became world famous. There is even a miniature train for children to take rides.

Stationary engines on display and at work in the Joiners' Shop

Wortley Arms Hotel

Wortley Village,
Sheffield.
Tel: 0144 2882245

Located at charming Wortley Village, a few minutes drive from the historic Wortley Forge, the Wortley Arms Hotel is a classic country Inn with inglenook fireplace. Comfortable,en suite rooms are available and dining ranges from sandwiches and bar snacks to a la carte. The Hotel is famous for its bar, well stocked with traditional ales and the widest range of malt whiskey in the area.

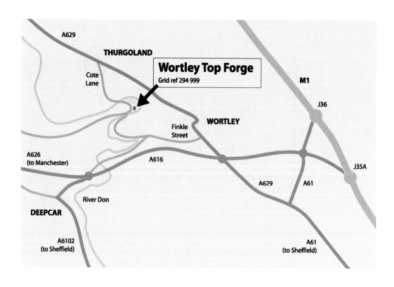

Cultural Industries
Quarter
Sheffield

For information
please contact:

CIQ Agency,
The Workstation,
15, Paternoster Row,
Sheffield S1 2BX

Tel: 0114 2490655

www.ciq.org.uk

Photography by iD.8

183

The 19th century Butcher's works, Arundel Street

The name Sheffield on steel products was once the badge of excellence throughout the world for cutlery and edged tools ranging from the humble garden spade to place settings for the tables of the rich and famous.

As the Industrial Revolution unfolded, Britain led the world in steel making and Sheffield led Britain in the making of such a variety of products that it would be true to say that no house would have been without several, including the basic scissors, knives, screwdrivers and other household tools.

Although Sheffield had a long history of cutlery production it was not until the Industrial Revolution brought canals and, most importantly, railways, to the landlocked city that its rise to international fame began in earnest. Also, it was not until 1856 that Henry Bessemer's converter enabled the mass production of steel. Until then, Sheffield's cutlery was made in relatively small quantities in hundreds of small furnaces.

The industry was located not only in Sheffield but in its outlying villages with different areas often specializing in certain products. Prior to the second decade of the 19th century, processes requiring power would be located along one of Sheffield's five rivers. But once the use of steam became widespread factories could be located more conveniently in the city centre close to suppliers, allied trades and transport infrastructure. Stages of production were integrated. But, as had been the case in almost all other industries, the cottage industry beginnings of Sheffield steel were embraced by the new factories with self employed workmen known as 'Little Mesters' renting space in these large works rather as stall-holders do in a modern market.

Factories and workshops crowded along the grids of streets which had been characteristic of Sheffield's urban development since the late 18th century. During its heyday in the late 19th and early 20th centuries downtown Sheffield was

Below: Putting the finishing touches to a piece of famous Sheffield cutlery.
Right: the kind of irons grandma used to sweat over - made in Sheffield.

densely developed and supported a vibrant community of cutlery manufacturers and related skilled metal workers, many living as well as working within the area. But, as the tides of development unleashed by the Industrial Revolution eventually receded and change and modernization swept through Sheffield's industries, whole sectors of the city fell into dereliction and decay. World War II bombing and road building and housing projects led to extensive clearances.

In the 1980s Sheffield City Council took steps to develop one such under-utilized area in the south west of the city, today known as the Cultural Industries Quarter, a few minutes walk from the bustling city centre. The CIQ, as it is known, is a regeneration project which began in 1982 and aimed to convert dereliction to dynamism through public/private sector cooperation which has resulted in a constantly enriching mix of public facilities such as Hallam University's City Centre Campus and hundreds of new small businesses. The CIQ is now a recognized business location for culture, science, technology, plating and cutlery based industries.

The 10-year vision for the CIQ is that it "will be a thriving cultural production zone, with more than 4,000 jobs in the cultural industries. The CIQ will have become a regionally - and in some cases nationally - significant centre for cultural activity and experience, and a destination in its own right. The CIQ will be established as a centre of excellence for creativity and knowledge creation, a model learning community for the new century."

The CIQ already offers a rich and diverse cultural experience for Sheffielders and visitors including a cluster of quality private and subsidized art galleries.Visual artists and crafts people enjoy a unique creative environment in the Persistence Works. The CIQ also offers popular art, cinema, live music and comedy in a variety of venues including the Leadmill all-night zone. The CIQ is a place to be enjoyed and experienced at all hours: cafes, restaurants, pubs and clubs.

But the area still represents a unique example of a specific form of industrial heritage that was tied to the tradition

Bringing yesteryear back to life: a film crew at work

of the 'Little Mesters.' These craftsmen in cutlery and tool making operated on a small scale and typically occupied plots and buildings that were in multiple use as workshops and often provided not only work space but dwellings as well.

Key examples of the original leasehold plots and of the courtyard building forms within them, which housed early industries, can be found throughout the area together with later examples of the evolution of these building types. Leases granted on properties in the late 1790s reveal that plots were subdivided so that plots envisaged for one individual property often developed into two or three buildings with residential accommodation at the front and workshops at the rear.

This form of development was typically grouped around courtyards and there are a number of early examples at the eastern end of Arundel Street, for example, the plot on the corner of Arundel Street and Howard Street, which was leased in 1796 to Richard Jessop, a silver plater, and on which he built two houses with workshops.

The years of the late 18th century were boom times across the Atlantic in what came to be known in 1776 as the United States of America. American independence sent shivers down the spines of Sheffield manufacturers. "The settler needed his axe to fell the primeval forest, his spade to break the hitherto un-tilled ground, his saw and chisel and file and scythe and shears for constant use in building and agriculture, as well as the necessary domestic utensils in setting up a new home." These were the very things for which Sheffield was becoming famous and a number of manufacturers were as well known in America as they were in Britain. Sheffield's suppliers had another century before they needed to seriously worry about erosion of their North American market as development enabled the United States to cater increasingly to its own needs.

On Arundel Street there is an example of one of the most successful businesses of the American boom years, still in its unchanged state from the beginning of the 19th century. William Butcher was born in Sheffield in about 1791, the son of a cutler. He and his brother Samuel entered the trade in 1819 when they decided to acquire a warehouse, workshop and yard in Eyre Lane. They produced a wide variety of steel goods including edge tools, skates, saws, files, hoes and trowels.

By 1822 they were melting their own crucible steel and during the prosperous 1830s the Butcher plant was greatly extended. These were boom years in the American trade and the company had so much business that it opened an office in New York headed by Robert Wade, an arrangement that led to the firm's goods being stamped "Wade and Butcher." Many New England manufacturers proudly advertised their products as being made of "W & S Butcher's superior refined cast steel." Commented one American: " The fame of the brothers Butcher is as widespread as commerce itself."

In 1835 the Butchers took the opportunity to expand further by adding the neighbouring tool and steel works of Mitchell Brothers & Co., in Furnival Street thus positioning themselves to participate in the great era of expansion of Sheffield's American trade during the 1850s and 60s. William

Butcher made a small fortune from the trade in Bowie knives alone.

Such was the huge potential of the American market that we find him not only selling his products but recruiting workmen for the Pennsylvania Steel Company in Harrisburg and in 1865, supervising the building of several Bessemer converters for producing bulk steel. That year he went to Philadelphia to plan the erection of his own steel works for the purpose of producing cast steel tyres for railway locomotives as well as heavy forgings and cast rails. The great American railway boom which would do so much to speed up the country's development and bind the country together from coast to coast was about to create a new generation of millionaires.

Like so many other developments in so many other countries the development of the American steel industry had its origins among the islands of Britain, in the case of steel, at the town of Sheffield on the slopes of the beautiful Pennines where local genius once turned the sky black with the smoke of its smithies and furnaces enabling its reputation as the centre of the cutlery and edge tool industries to be carried to the four corners of the globe.

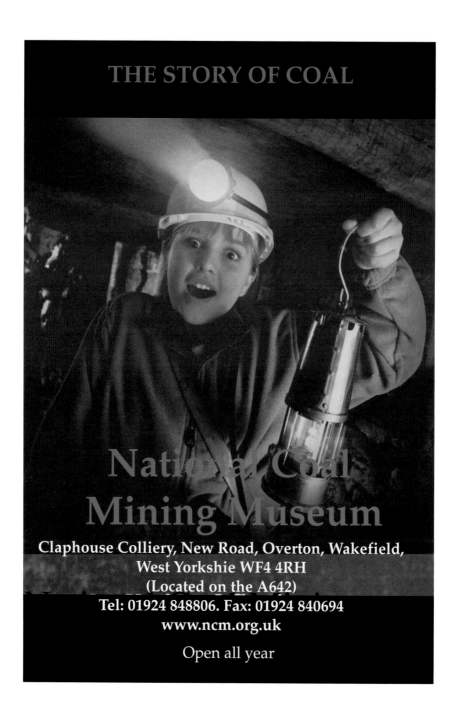

Most people generally have a vague idea that coal is mined in dark tunnels far underground. But did you know that the subterranean workers included children as young as seven, that girls and women used to work below ground as well as on the surface moving heavy tubs of coal and sorting coal from dust and that in the 19th century more than 70,000 ponies worked alongside the people hundreds of feet below the surface?

When you start to look into it there's far more to coal mining than just digging a hole. And mining had social consequences which led to the creation of whole communities and to a specific way of life in the mining areas.

The National Coal Mining Museum at Caphouse Colliery was a working colliery until 1985 and the shaft where visitors descend today is probably the earliest coal mining shaft still in use in Britain. The earliest evidence of a shaft at Caphouse dates from 1791. The Colliery is considered to be the best preserved 19th century pit anywhere in the United Kingdom.

Small wonder that in 1988 the Colliery became the Yorkshire Mining Museum and in 1995 the National Coal Mining Museum for England. Many of the old pit buildings have been restored, new galleries have been built and in the long term there are ambitious plans to augment the collections as well as to improve public accessibility and enjoyment through the re-introduction of the railway which once ran through the mine grounds.

Caphouse is still treated as a working colliery with daily inspections to verify that conditions in the shafts and tunnels are safe. Every year thousands of visitors follow former miners on tours 140 metres (439 feet) underground to discover for themselves the secrets so long unknown in the ground beneath their feet.

The underground tour traces mining techniques and conditions through time. It starts in the 19th century when women and children still worked underground in the dust and semi-darkness, often forming family based teams. Visitors see how ponies were used before machines were introduced until

modern times when mining became a much more automated process relying on brains more than brawn.

The lamp room at Caphouse looks as if the miners have just left it at the end of a shift and it is from here that visitors enter a cage or lift to descend to a now nearly forgotten world far below.

It is often said that without an abundance of relatively easily recoverable coal as well as unique proximity to waterborne transport Great Britain's early industrial development may have happened quite differently and not nearly so fast.

The National Coal Mining Museum is not just another pit to have fun going down but a Museum founded to tell the story of coal.

The story of coal is not just about a black mineral and its extraction but about the men and women who did the work - and enjoyed what they could of their leisure.

Mining communities were famous for galas, sport, brass bands and shows which were part of community life. Sport played a huge role and many famous footballers, rugby players and cricketers had their roots in mining areas. The Colliery often sponsored pit teams and many leisure activities were supported by the Miners' Welfare Fund. As well as high days and holidays there were bitter spells of unemployment and fierce battles between the miners' trade unions and the employers before nationalisation in 1947. "There's trouble at pit or at mill" were almost bywords of the earlier phases of British industrial development.

Interactive displays and exhibitions at the Museum's visitor centre explain what coal is and why it was once important. And through audio-visual plasma screens in the Mining Lives Gallery the lives of the miners and their

families below ground and above are brought vividly to life.

Preserved buildings at the Caphouse site include the coal screening plant, the steam winding engine house and the pithead baths built only in 1938, more than a century after the colliery was built in 1830.

It is hard to imagine the actual life of miners at various times in the industry's long history.

Coal Interface1 is a gallery showing the cramped, noisy and dirty conditions in which miners worked as well as some of the hazards of working underground. There is an opportunity to see some of the problems they had to deal with and to try to solve them yourself. Fascinatingly, there are displays of some of the enormous machines which eventually came to be used both for cutting coal and making mine roadways. One cutting drum weighs an incredible 39 tonnes. The Museum is home to a large and ever growing collection of mining machines.

Coal Interface II shows the importance of coal, its effect on the environment and its future. Britain's mining areas were often very different because of local conditions and each coal mining region is given an area in the Gallery.

A coal mine always has a large part of its operations and its workforce above ground, processing the coal won from the depths below. Today, when visitors yearn again for the bright sunlight after a tour of the pit, they can enjoy a ride on the Paddy Train which runs from one end of the large site to the other, providing panoramic views of the colliery superstructure. These man-riding trains were once used underground and the Paddy Train uses a rope haulage system driven by a haulage engine.

There is also a Nature Trail running along the western boundary of the site, passing through a range of flora and fauna, including woodland, marsh and cleared areas.

A new cafeteria looks out onto spectacular views across the valley to Thornhill Edge and the gift shop is rich in publications and souvenirs of coal mining. The Museum naturally attracts many school and educational visitors and in addition to its primary role is also a conference centre.

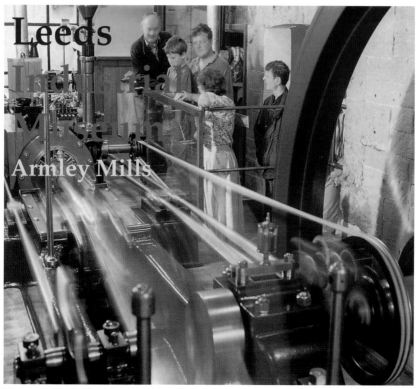

Leeds
Industrial
Museum
Armley Mills

Photographs in this chapter © Leeds Museums & Galleries

L eeds Industrial Museum at Armley Mills
aims to tell as much as possible about the
people, manufacturing and commerce
which associated Leeds with the varied and rapid growth
characteristic of the unfolding Industrial Revolution, particularly
as it spilled over into the 19th century.

Situated between the hill farms of the Pennines
and the crop producing areas of the East Riding of Yorkshire,
Leeds has a long history of involvement in the wool trade, a
history which in the 19th century would see its skyline dotted
with tall mill chimneys spewing forth the black soot and ash with
which all its buildings were eventually grimed.

In the age before steam the only form of power

available other than human muscles or horse power was wind or water power. Water power was the most favoured. The natural flow of rivers and streams was used to turn wheels immersed in them and these in turn provided relatively stable power for such activities as corn grinding, cloth fulling and wool spinning.

The River Aire at Armley, Leeds, was chosen as an ideal site for these activities because at this point the river ran wide and deep and was capable of turning any number of water wheels from the largest to the smallest.

The earliest record of milling at Armley dates from the middle of the 16th century but in 1788, by which time the Industrial Revolution and factory production was well under way, Armley Mills was bought by a Colonel Thomas Lloyd.

The structure of Britain's textile industry was changing. There was a move away from traditional cloths and markets to lighter fabrics and newer and more far flung markets. Lloyd rebuilt the mills making them into not only Britain's largest fulling mills but the biggest fulling mills in the world. He then leased them to Israel and John Burrows who had two semi-detached houses built above the Leeds and Liverpool Canal which can still be seen today. Visitors can contrast the life-style of the managers with reconstructions of the living quarters of working class weavers. As is still the case today, we can easily see that money bought everything.

In 1804 a wool merchant named Benjamin Gott agreed to buy Armley Mills from Lloyd beginning a process which would send his name ringing down the corridors of industrial history. In November, 1805, the mill was almost entirely destroyed by fire and Gott decided to rebuild. The old building had been made from stone and wood but Gott was able to use the latest technology rebuilding in fireproof brick and iron. The remnants of the old 18th century mill can still be seen with Gott's construction sitting on top, by itself a tribute to the progress of the Industrial Revolution.

Gott's incentive to buy the mill was the scale of embezzlement of materials to which he was subjected by the cottage workers he supplied. It would be significantly more

The clothing gallery

efficient and profitable if the spinning of the wool he required could be undertaken under one roof. It is Gott's building that the visitor sees today. Armley Mills prospered under Gott's management, exporting its wares to North and South America, Europe and the Far East. In 1801 there were about 20 factories in Leeds, not all engaged in textiles, but by 1838 there were 106 woollen mills alone. Gott became one of the largest and wealthiest employers in Britain.

Armley Mills today is rich in the atmosphere of Gott's days. The relatively large and noisy machines which carded, spun and warped the yarn look fascinatingly intricate to the modern eye with all their parts and workings exposed like utilities on the outside of a hyper-modern building. Into one such machine in 1822 tumbled young George Dyson, his life cruelly snuffed out at the age of only 13. In the textile industries as a whole, women and children made up a significant part of the workforce. The years hide from our view the poverty in which the workers of these boom times lived and the appalling conditions in which many of them worked. After a succession of owners, the mills finally closed in 1969 and were bought by Leeds City Council for use as an industrial museum.

The demand for machinery and equipment used by the textile industry created opportunities for engineers in Leeds and during the 19th century locomotives, cranes, traction engines and other heavy engineering products were exported around the globe. The Industrial Museum displays a range of these machines, often lovingly restored to working order ranging from a stationary mill engine to a mobile ploughing engine.

The Burrows brothers and Benjamin Gott were not the only men to make Armley Mills and Leeds famous. It was in this city that the ready-to-wear industry was born. The inspiration behind this new industry destined to take the world by storm was John Barran.

In the 1850s Barran applied new technology to the industry introducing Singer sewing machines and, more innovatively, a new type of band knife made by Leeds engineers Greenwood and Batley. Visitors can stroll through sewing rooms arranged as they would have been in Barran's day The lines of female machinists face to face across a workbench have to be imagined but photographs help. There are also displays of the kind of jackets, trousers, blouses, shirts, dresses and even hats made here and destined to be bought "off the peg" from shops around Britain and the world. The ready-to-wear industry flourished involving a number of companies which later became household names, such as Burtons and Hepworths. The big clothing factories were supplemented by large numbers of sweatshops where Jewish immigrants driven from Russia and Poland after 1881 provided a cheap workforce. The importance of the industry can be gauged from the fact that by 1911 a quarter of women workers in Leeds were employed in the clothing industry.

Another major Leeds industry in the early 20th century was printing and by 1911 it was the fourth largest in the city employing 8,000 people. A Printing Gallery at the museum includes a reconstructed printer's workshop. One famous Leeds printing company was John Waddington Limited, best known for its game 'Monopoly.'

Kalee cameras and cine projectors were made in Leeds and there is a fully operational cinema of the 1920s in the museum showing many old films of the period from a projection roomwhich includes original Kalee equipment.

Not all the exhibits are inside. In the grounds visitors can come across the huge Benjamin Hick's beam engine, the world's first automatic traffic light; the world's first commercially built diesel locomotive, produced in the 1930s and a bright-as-a-button steam locomotive 'Jack' built in 1898 and still running.

Because Armley Mills seeks to reflect the full gamut of industrial activities which made up Leeds' busy past the museum is a place of great variety and interest with each new gallery revealing something new and exciting to the visitor. Armley Mills is one of the most "atmospheric" of all Britain's industrial heritage museums, its sandstone buildings cleaving close to the River Aire on one side and the Leeds and Liverpool Canal on the other. If they are lucky a narrow boat may be sailing past, recalling the days when barges stopped here to pick up cargoes that might be shipped around the world.

Please call for opening times and admission charges

Tel: 0113 263 7861

Armley Mills, Canal Road, Leeds LS12 2QF

Queen Street Mill Museum & Helmshore Textile Museums

Few sights are more evocative of the Industrial Revolution than the Weaving Shed at Queen Street Mill, Harle Syke, Burnley, built in 1894.

To enter the Weaving Shed is a huge step back in time - to the days when veritable armies of workers toiled at their machines and when, for the first time in history, a single giant steam engine could provide power for hundreds of machines.

In the Weaving Shed there are over 300 traditional steam-powered Lancashire looms, one next to another, each one identical to the last, standing on the hard flagstone floor. The floor had to be able to stand the weight of the looms and the vibration of the mechanisms. The cast iron beams holding up the roof also had to support the line shafts and drums and take the strain of the belt drives which operate the looms.

'Cloned' machines like this were the very essence of the Industrial Revolution. In the days before the factory system spinners and weavers worked from home and increases in output were limited. Within a few years, a whole new class of workers was called into existence as the factory system and its

©Lancashire County Museums

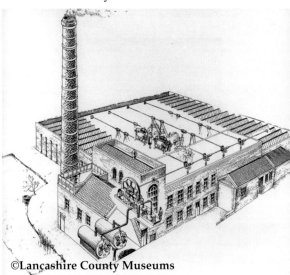

©Lancashire County Museums

Above: A demonstration in the Weaving Shed at Queens Street Mill.

Left: A diagram showing the layout of the mill with the Weaving Shed, steam engine, boilers and Lancashire looms marked clearly.

machines drove up output prodigiously, helping Britain achieve its reputation as the 'Workshop of the World'.

In the 19th century Lancashire was home to hundreds of mills. The industry reached its peak just before the First World War when Burnley alone had over 100,000 looms. Today Queen Street Mill is the only working steam powered weaving mill left in Britain - and, indeed, the world.

Queen Street Mill is remarkable not only for its survival as a museum but because it survived until 1982 as a workers' co-operative. The idea behind the co-operative was that workers should "obtain a greater interest in the results of their labour." Whole families invested in the mill.

At first, the motive power driving the hundreds of looms in the Weaving Shed is invisible to the visitor who sees only machines linked by belts to rotating overhead shafts. The noise and clatter of the looms is deafening and, indeed, the fate of many of the hands who once toiled here was to suffer deafness. Noise levels were so high that workers learned to lip read and even to use sign language. Most of the weaving was done by women and girls but men and boys kept the weaving machines running.

Today, the looms are run only for demonstration purposes but real cloth is made and as a result an exclusive textile range " Simply Textiles" is available at the museum shop.

The secret of what powers the 300 looms is eventually revealed. The Engine House accommodates the 1894 steam engine 'Peace,' so christened after the 1914-18 war in which tens of thousands of lives were sometimes lost in an hour of battle on the flat plains of France. Steam engines like 'Peace' were rarely seen by the men and women who worked in the mills with only the very privileged being allowed in to the engine room.

'Peace' has been maintained in immaculate condition to the extent that it is hard to imagine that it is a mere mill workhorse. At a time when the age of steam is long past its shiny tubes and whirling governor are an irreplaceable fascination. You can watch the stoker shovel coal into the flames of the Lancashire boiler that powers 'Peace.' Once upon a time

Above: In the 'Revolution' gallery at Helmshore, Arkwright's Water Frame, built about 1785. This is the only complete 96-spindle Water Frame in the world.
Inset, 'Peace' the mighty engine that drives the Weaving Shed's 300 looms.

Photographs©Lancashire County Museums

there were much larger steam engines than 'Peace' but at 500 hp, 'Peace' has no difficulty providing the motive power for 300 tireless looms and other mill equipment besides.

Queen Street Mill provides visitors with a fairly complete explanation of the weaving process. On the way out of the Engine House a beaming frame shows the first stages of assembling many strands of yarn into a beam. As you enter the mill a cylinder sizing machine shows how the warp threads are strengthened by the addition of "size," a mixture of flour, soap and tallow to form the warp threads running along the length of the cloth. This single machine can supply up to 400 looms. Opposite, two banks of pirn winders show how weft is wound - weft is the yarn that goes across the warp in the shuttle. Naturally, there were a great many beams and a special room was needed known as a drawing-in room which visitors can enter today and see how the work was done.

Queen Street Mill provides a home to a unique collection of looms including the Hattersley, built for the Franco-British Exhibition of 1908 and which only ever wove a single pattern throughout its entire life - a design based on a painting by Landseer called Bolton Abbey in ye olden times.

Adults and children alike are mesmerized by the display of industrial might still working at Queen Street Mill as it was a century ago. Hands on programmes show children what it was like to work in the Mill in the 1960s, including role-playing.

There is a regular programme of visitor events at the mill and the gift shop stocks a wide range of publications telling more of the story of Lancashire textiles and of the Industrial Revolution. The Weavers' Rest Cafe is a cozy place for a cup of tea.

Helmshore Textile Museums, nestled in the undiscovered beauty of the Rossendale Valley, consists of two former mills, Higher Mill, built in 1789 as a woollen fulling mill and the larger Whitaker's Mill, constructed during the 1820s for the carding, spinning and weaving of wool. A hundred years later, Whitaker's Mill was being operated as a condenser cotton plant, a role continued until its closure in 1978.

A great deal of cotton waste was available in Lancashire and the Mill used this waste to make soft full yarn which could be used as weft - the yarn carried by the shuttle. Many types of cotton fabric could be made using cotton waste including sheeting, flannelettes, cheap towels and cleaning cloths. Examples of the machines which processed this waste starting with the preparing machinery which first received the cotton waste and finishing with the Condenser Cotton Mules, which spun the yarn, can be seen immediately after leaving the Revolution Gallery close to the museum entrance and also on the first floor of Whitaker's Mill. The condenser cotton spinning room on this level is an almost unique example of an early textile workplace, very much as it would have been when in operation.

In the 'Revolution' gallery, thanks to modern electronics, visitors can 'meet' Richard Arkwright, one of the pioneers of Britain's industrialised textile industry. It is easy to

©Lancashire County Museum

All our yesterdays - mill girls take a break to pose for the camera. Women and girls did the weaving but men and boys kept the looms running.

Above: One of two stocks dated 1849 and a 5.5 metre diameter water wheel at Higher Mill Museum.

believe that we are really listening to the Lancashire inventor as he explains what brought about his inventions. John Kay, James Hargreaves and Samual Crompton are also present in the gallery.

Here too we can see examples of some of the inventions themselves, such as Richard Arkwright's famous Water Frame, so called because it was powered by a water wheel turned by the fast flowing currents of the rivers of the Derwent Valley and important because its use marked the beginning of the factory system. The Water Frame on display was made circa 1785 and was taken from his famous mill at Cromford. It is also the only complete production machine of its type in the world.

Arkwright realized that the mass production potential of his invention would be lost if he did not mechanise all the processes prior to spinning. Cottage workers disentangled and straightened fibres using bats covered with fine wire pins but Arkwright was able to invent rotary carding engines. The fibre was introduced in the form of a continuous lap and carded cotton removed by a crank and comb. The Lap Forming Machines, carding engines and draw frames on display in the 'Revolution' gallery are all originals from Cromford Mill.

The combination of machinery and electronic presentations at Whitaker's Mill and Higher Mill lures the visitor deep into the story of Lancashire's textile industry from 1750 to the eve of the First World War. The displays tell a story and like all stories we want to know what happens next. We are inducted into the lives of ordinary weavers and not just those of the rich and famous.

These riveting displays are complemented by periodic imaginative Bringing History Alive performances at special events throughout the season. Here visitors meet Croft and his sister back in 1826 or listen to Joy and Frank in the 1960s oblivious to the demolition gangs already beginning to put the infrastructure of the world famous industry under the wrecker's hammer. There are special educational programmes for school children incorporating all the fun of role- playing in which the children are shown what it would have been like to have worked at the mills long ago.

Higher Mill, Helmshore was built as a water powered fulling mill for the purpose of finishing woollen cloth, which had been woven in local cottages. It is still powered today by a magnificent waterwheel. Fulling is the process which produces a controlled shrinkage and thickening of woven woollen cloth. A somewhat similar effect can be produced at home by putting a woollen garment into very hot water or leaving it wet for too long.

A water wheel was very suitable for driving the fulling stocks which were required to run for long periods but which used only a modest amount of power. The present double rim geared wheel was installed in the late 1840s. The internally toothed rim gear drove the tappet shaft for the stocks at about 13 rpm. An externally toothed rim gear and a compound gear train produced about 150 rpm at the line shafting which drove all the other machines in the mill. None of the surviving machinery seems to be earlier than 1849. The Mill was completely

The spectacular spinning floor at Helmshore Textile Museums
Photograph ©Lancashire County Museums

re-equipped at least once since its construction in 1789 and much of this machinery remained in place until the Mill's closure in 1967.

For opening times and admission charges please contact:

Helmshore Textile Museums,
Holcombe Road,
Helmshore,
Rossendale,
Lancashire BB4 4NP
Tel: 01706 226459
Fax: 01706 218554
Email: helmshore.museums
@mus.lancscc.gov.uk

Queen Street Mill Museum,
Harle Street,
Burnley, BB10 2HX.
Tel: 01282 412555. Fax: 01282 430220.
Email:
queenstreet.mill@mus.lancscc.gov.uk

Beeties

BAR-RESTAURANT-BEDROOMS

7, Victoria Road,
Saltaire Village,
Shipley,
BD18 3LA.
Tel: 01274 595988

Email: enquiries@beeties.co.uk
Website: www.beeties.co.uk
This tastefully restored and converted
grade two listed Victorain building is
located in the heart of the Saltaire World
Heritage Site, within walking distance of
Salt's Mill. All rooms en suite. Warmth,
comfort and hospitality from the moment
you arrive. Modern dining, Tapas and
Wine bar on the premises. Awarded one
AA rosette.

Apollo Canal Cruises

Shipley Wharf,
Wharf Street,
Shipley,
BD17 7DW
Tel: 01274 595914

website: www.apollocanalcruises.co.uk
All year round daytime and evening
cruises along the Leeds and Liverpool
Canal, one of the major arteries of the
Industrial Revolution. Visitors embark at
a wharf at the heart of the Saltaire World
Heritage Site, overlooked by the massive
Salt's Mill. Cruises of differing durations
offer visitors a choice of a short ride or a
longer voyage.

Saltaire
World
Heritage
Site

Shipley
West Yorkshire

Titus Salt's mill at Shipley, West Yorkshire, is gargantuan, looking like some huge, land based, stone, Titanic. Its enormous bulk expresses the capability, the power and the self assurance of the Industrial Revolution. The length of this cathedral of industry matches that of St Paul's and its chimney rises spire-like to a height of nearly 80 metres above its six storeys. The top storey was once a single room and in the 1850s had the reputation of being the largest and longest in the world. At the opening ceremony in 1853 the Mayor of Bradford was reported as saying: " We have built a palace of industry almost equal to the palaces of the Caesars."

On completion of the mill, work turned to the construction of a village around it.. Houses, public baths and washhouses, its hospital, church, almshouses, chapel, workmen's institute and park were all built around a steam-powered mill served by the Leeds & Liverpool Canal and by the Midland Railway. The model village was named Saltaire, after Titus Salt, its founder and the River Aire that flows through the site. Mill and village were built so solidly that even today the thousands of workers who laboured in the works or lived in any of its 820 houses during the closing decades of the 19th century would have no diffculty in recognising the place.

So much a monument to a particular phase and process of the Industrial Revolution has Saltaire become that it has achieved the designation of a World Heritage Site. It exemplifies the culmination of the development of model industrial villages. Indeed, Salt himself intended the complex to be a model for the new Industrial Age.

Experts say that the structure of Saltaire evolved rather than being designed in entirety. The building took place against the back drop of an ongoing discussion about the living conditions and education of the working class and men like Titus Salt saw a link between healthy, temperate and educated workers and a profitable business. The village surrounding the mill reflects not arrogance but an employer's care for his workforce uncharacteristic of much of the 18th century but more prevalent

after the second quarter of the 19th, when municipal officials and the national government were realizing that social conditions had to be improved and were driving forward reforms. Bradford was something of a vision from hell and the life span of the average person was relatively short, more two score years and ten than the norm of the later inter-world war years of three score years and ten. Salt was not the first to identify the employer's model village as a solution to the problem of maintaining a healthy and happy workforce at a time when poverty, ignorance and drunkenness were common in fast growing industrial villages. He continued a tradition, but the range of facilities provided and the architectural harmony of the buildings at Saltaire are exemplary and won much acclaim at the time of construction. The idea of moving the population out of town centres to more spacious, attractive and healthy surroundings was to be instrumental in the evolution of town planning into the 20th century.

Salt was also a religious man with a strong sense of right and wrong. Philanthropy and compassion are words often used to describe him but Salt was no spendthrift. He was a careful man with money and bringing Saltaire to reality was undertaken on a strictly cost-effective basis and with an eye to improved workforce quality and management. Salt knew the value of money, the swings of the pendulum of business and the penalties for failure. He hailed from a family of entrepreneurs and showed no reluctance to get into business himself - doubtless inspired by the example of his father whose aim is said to have been to make as much money as possible.

By the time Salt was aged 21 he had joined his father running a firm engaged in buying and selling wool, with the energetic, young, son taking the lead and setting the pace. One consignment he purchased came from the Don River region of Russia and was so coarse that there were no buyers. Salt thought that it could be spun, experimented and proved his point. In 1836 chance led him to discover Peruvian alpaca and his unique success in spinning that enabled him to amass the fortune which financed his mill and village at Saltaire. Salt's business success had led him to own five mills in Bradford and tremendous economies of scale would be achieved if all the operations could be unified under one roof as he achieved at Salt's Mill.

The colossal Saltaire Mill, the United Reform Church, the almshouses for the destitute and Salt's schools and Institute are built in a regal Italianate style Salt much admired. The buildings are a mixture of formal beauty and of a solidness which suggests that their destiny is to remain standing long after their creator has passed away. Lest too many forget, Titus Salt's initials can be found sprinkled liberally in stone throughout the village.

To stroll around Saltaire today is to be in the presence of Titus Salt. After all, he is why we are there. His quest for money through entrepreneurial activities makes him a very modern man to whom we can easily relate. And in an age of extreme individualism it is not hard to understand the impulses which led to the grandiose scale of his creation nor the inscription of his initials wherever possible.

The Salt's connection with the Mill and the village lasted only 41 years during which time the father and the one son who had shown interest in continuing the business died and the properties passed into new hands. The village ceased to be a company village in 1933 at which time the houses were sold to the Bradford Property Trust Company and subsequently to individual owners. The significance of the village was recognised in 1971 when it was designated as a conservation area by the local authority. However, with the decline of Britain's textile industry in the 1980s many of the major buildings in the village fell into dereliction and the enclave's future seemed bleak.

In 1984, the Saltaire Village Society was formed to fight for the conservation and restoration of the village and a year later English Heritage listed most of the buildings of the village, acknowleding their historic and architectuiral interest and affrding them some statutory protection. In 1987, Jonathan Silver, a local businessman, bought Salt's mill. He established the 1853 Art Gallery, featuring pictures by artist, David Hockney and the same year embarked on ventures that has made the mill the attraction it is today, with art galleries, shops and restaurants and an unusual and ambitious programme of cultural events, including theatre. The gave the village a new lease of life and spurred its regeneration. Over time, the other buildings became owned or tenanted by offices, factories and shops and the village houses filled up with young professionals who could easily commute to Bradford and Leeds from the station. Shops along Victoria Road were revitalised, benefiting from the increasing number of visitors to the village. The canal towpath provides an attractive walking or cycling experience and visitors can take rides in canal boats and even dine by its sides. Across Robert's Park which was also laid out as part of the industrial village and contains a number of sporting facilities, and the River Aire, a cable car carries visitors to the picturesque Shipley Glen on the edge of the moors where the striking setting of this unique village can be truly appreciated.

The ornate
United
Reform
Church -
Titus Salt
lies
within.

National Railway Museum

THE STORY OF THE TRAIN

Leeman Road,
York YO26 4XJ
Tel: 01904 621261
Facsimile: 01904 611112
Email: nrm@nmsi.ac.uk
Website: www.nrm.org.uk

OPEN ALL YEAR

At the beginning of the 21st century, it is hard to believe the extent to which, a hundred and sixty years ago, rail travel revolutionized the movement of freight and people. In the process, rail travel changed the way of life forever, not only of Britons, but of people around the world.

Although we read about rail mania in the 1830s and 40s, the development of the railways proceeded rather slowly and its imperative was not the transport of passengers but of heavy goods, particularly coal and iron. Throughout the second half of the 18th century, canals were used for this purpose and horses hauled heavy wooden trams to the nearest 'cut.'

Up to three hundred years earlier, in mines around Europe, it was human muscle-power that had pushed along trucks full of coal, often with a hanging metal pin which slotted in between two wooden planks, thus guiding them along. A replica of one of these very early wagons can be seen in the Museum.

The first waggonways in Britain appeared in Nottingham in 1600, spreading north to Tyneside and west to the Severn Valley. Early rails were made of wood but, once cast iron became cheaper, iron rails began to appear, enabling heavier loads to be carried. At first, the iron rails were flanged and the wheels smooth. Over time, rails became smooth and wooden wheels became iron hooped and eventually wholly iron and flanged, as they are today.

MIRACLE OF THE AGE

Steam had been used as early as 1698 to drive pumping engines but it would be almost a hundred years more before James Watt invented the rotary steam engine. Together with Matthew Boulton, the two men began to manufacture steam engines on a relatively large scale for a rapidly widening range of uses. One of these uses was driving moving engines to replace the horses which had for so long trodden the tramways and tow paths of Britain. Fixed steam engines had been tried with limited

success and examples such as the 'Weatherhill' and the 'Leicester & Swannington' engines can be seen in the Museum's Great Hall. miracle of the age, promising not only power but motion, a concept in its way comparable to flying to the moon. At first, the train hardly out-paced the horse drawn mail coach and it was common for a man with a red flag to walk in front to warn the public of approaching danger. It was not speed that was being sought but power and it is this that steam steadily delivered.

The first successful moving or locomotive steam engine was Richard Trevithick's in 1804. Initially there was much public cynicism about the likelihood of the 'iron horse's' success and many teething problems until the 1830s by which time George Stephenson had invented his 'Locomotion' and 'Rocket' and Timothy Hackworth his rival 'Sanspareil' and 'Royal George.' When the world's first railway opened at Stockton & Darlington in 1825 horses were still used to pull the trains. The new locos so frequently broke down that there were serious doubts about their future.

In 1829, when the first inter-city line was being built from Manchester to Liverpool, the directors of the company put out a challenge. They offered a purse of £500 to anyone able to better the existing locomotives. The requirement was for an engine to pull three times its own weight only one-and-three-quarter miles of track forty times at an average speed of 10 mph. The contest took place in front of thousands of spectators at Rainhill in 1829 and there were several competitors. Stephenson's Rocket achieved speeds of 13 mph and won amid allegations that Timothy Hackworth's rival 'Sanspareil' had been sabotaged. The Museum's replica Rocket shows why Stephenson was judged the winner. His innovations included making the boiler more effective, improving the fire and improving the driving mechanism. The original Rocket can be seen at the Science Museum in London.

Britain built an incredible 110,000 locomotives between 1804 and 1971 and some of the most famous are on display at the Museum, including the 'Stirling Single,' the 'Chinese Locomotive', 'Ellerman Lines' and the 'Mallard.' Among its large collection, the very last steam locomotive to be built for British Railways, the 'Evening Star' can also be seen, painted as a passenger locomotive despite its being dual use and with a copper-capped chimney and a special plaque to mark its status. Some of the old warriors can be seen running at the Museum while replicas provide fun rides for visitors.

Once the early engineering problems of locomotion were solved and steam technology developed, with the opening of the first passenger railway in 1835 linking Manchester and Liverpool, the door to railway mania was well and truly open. Whether it was to previously rarely visited neighbouring cities and even villages of Britain, the seemingly endless prairies of North America, the plains of India or the patchwork of states on the European continent, for the first time in history, those who could afford it were now virtually 'as free as a bird.' Soon, they would be able to cross the world entirely by train.

Goods could not only be taken more easily and cheaply to market but the products and produce of far away markets could be brought back. This drove trade statistics up to record levels and the populations of whole towns, mushroomed around northern Britain. Stations, bridges and viaducts, sometimes of daring and even ornate proportions and architecture, changed the face of Britain. The plume of steam in the countryside, the shrill but lonely-sounding whistle, the hissing of the great engines as they came and went from one station to another in frothing clouds of steam - these were the essential images of the age of the steam train. Thanks to steam locomotion, men and women could move easily to find jobs in the burgeoning towns. Farmers, manufacturers and traders could do more business more often. News travelled faster as letters and newspapers were loaded onto trains for delivery around the country, diets improved and cheap fuel could be delivered to homes and factories. Life was being turned upside down. It was truly a new age.

For the next century, railwaymen were to be among the cream of Britain's industrial workers, their engines being built and cared for with the same kind of love and devotion lavished by steam enthusiasts today.

Nowhere in Britain tells the revolutionary story of the railways more fully and excitingly than the National Railway Museum at York. But the Museum is much more than a collection of locomotives, carriages, equipment, models, tickets or even railway advertising, often so redolent of those times of long hot summers, days at the seaside or excursions to the countryside. Over and beyond its fascinating and varied collections, the Museum tells a riveting story which, as it unfolds, shows us not only objects but the people who made them and the people who used them. It is part of the story of our lives.

And it is a story which has not yet finished. Just as we perhaps thought that the internal combustion engine and its marvel the car had consigned the train to the trash heap of history, new leaps in technology have been made and there is fresh interest in the train as a means of helping solve the growing congestion of highways and inter-city areas. In Britain, since 1993, privatization has brought about an explosion of new development and the Museum's trackside viewing balcony allows visitors to see some of this for themselves.

Gone are the shabby old green trains of British Railways and in their place a new generation of brightly coloured, comfortable, coaches pulled at high speed between hub stations brimming with retail outlets. On board an array of foods and even wines and spirits puts to shame the sloshing tea cups and cardboard sandwiches of yesteryear.

Perhaps the most spectacular of the train's recent victories has been its use in linking the British Isles with continental Europe by means of the thirty one mile long Channel Tunnel. To understand fully this incredible feat of engineering, visitors can take a look at the Channel Tunnel ring displayed in the Museum.

Modern trainaholics can see at the Museum not only the first trains and the fastest trains but also examples of

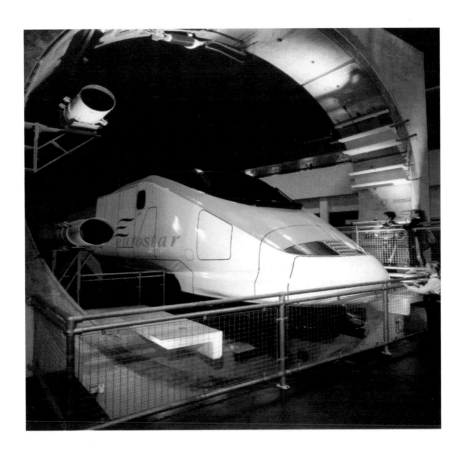

carriages deemed the most comfortable, such as the luxurious Pullmans "Golden Arrow' and 'Brighton Belle.' By the 1930s, sleeper carriages made possible train travel across the Channel, not under it, like today, but aboard specially built ferry boats and examples can be seen in the Museum. Once in France, passengers might get aboard the Orient Express and travel all the way to Vladivostock. They still can, today, in an age of resurgent rail travel, aboard the Trans-Siberian Express. VIPs could hire trains and the most important VIP family of all, the Royal Family, has often had its own. For those who wonder what a Royal train is like inside there is an opportunity to find out at the Museum where several Royal carriages are on display.

Railway advertising developed virtually into an art form of its own, tempting passengers to all the destinations they could reach by train. By the 1960s rail advertising moved away from destinations - which could then be reached by car - and focused more on the advantages of train travel. The Museum's collection of railway advertising is so vast that only a small part is on display but even that carries the visitor into an alluring world long gone. Copies of poster advertising can even be bought in the gift shop. Trains and art have always gone together and the Museum is home to an incredible one-and-a-quarter million images, regularly used by researchers and publishers and a selection is always available for the public to view.

There seems nothing about trains that the National Railway Museum doesn't have on display, including even jig saws, board games and toys. There is a model railway and even miniature railway rides. Because of its obvious expertise, the Museum has a reference library and an education service, including an Interactive Learning Centre for school children. For the casual visitor it's a wonderful day out at the railways.

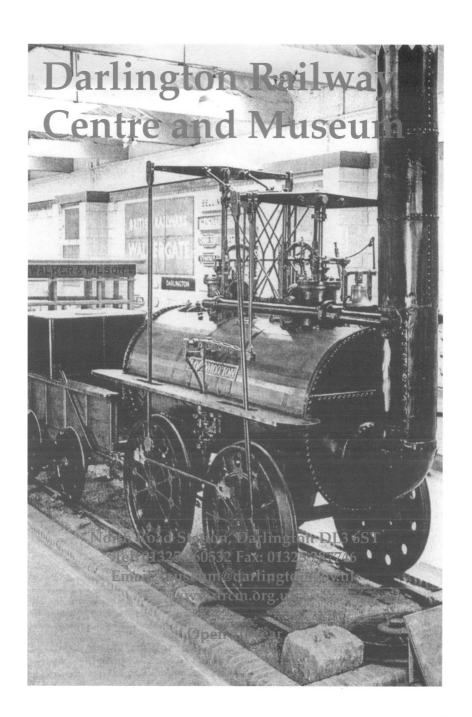

Darlington Railway Centre and Museum

North Road Station, Darlington DL3 6ST
Tel: 01325 460532 Fax: 01325 287746
Email: museum@darlington.gov.uk
www.drcm.org.uk

Open all year

Whether you are an ardent railway enthusiast, a tourist or a casual visitor, to enter Darlington Railway Centre and Museum is to step back in time.

Early 19th century experiments in the use of steam haulage on iron rails and the opening of the Stockton & Darlington Railway in 1825 heralded the birth of a revolutionary form of transport for goods and passengers.

Railways spread throughout the British Isles after 1825 and were a key part of the Industrial Revolution, speeding industrial and commercial development at home as well as having an impact in many other parts of the world. British engineers were to pioneer railways in many foreign countries.

North Road Station, where the Museum is located, is built on the original route of the Stockton & Darlington Railway, the world's first public steam railway, in an area often known as ' the cradle of the railways.'

The Stockton & Darlington Railway came about because of the need to link the south-west Durham coal field and the River Tees. Transporting the coal relied on horse-drawn wagons or pack horses, an unwieldy and expensive process.

THE RAILWAY AGE HAD BEGUN

For almost half a century surveys and estimates were made to effect the link by means of canal but funds were never forthcoming. Schemes for canals continued until 1818 when the latest suggestion threatened to bypass Darlington. The railway age had by now begun and the eventual result of the bypass threat was the first meeting of the Stockton & Darlington Railway Company in May, 1821.

George Stephenson was hired as the proposed line's surveyor and engineer. Stephenson was born at Wylam and his father worked at Wylam Colliery in the Northumberland coalfield. Two now famous engines were developed to haul coal from the colliery, the evocatively nameds 'Puffing Billy' and its companion the 'Wylam Dilley,' the first in the London Science

Recorded sounds of steaming and whistling make it seem as if the trains are still in service.

Museum and the second in Edinburgh's Royal Museum of Scotland.

The line on which these cranking, hissing, smoke spewing contraptions passed up and down every day ran right outside the Stephenson's family front door. The young Stephenson worked at the mine as an engine-wright and the need to make the engines more powerful and faster led him to make a number of improvements which soon spread his reputation far and wide.

By 1825, he was building his own engines and on September 27, 1825, Stephenson's 'Locomotion' became the first engine to pull trucks along the line and the famous loco can still be seen in the Museum close to where it once worked. The wagons carried directors and shareholders, bulk goods, especially coal, and 450 excited passengers rumbling along at 15 mph.

The growth of the Company was rapid and by 1839 it had 30 locomotives and many other lines had successfully

The 'Derwent,' the oldest surviving loco made at Darlington.

opened as railway mania swept the country.

The idea of purpose built stations developed slowly, partly because there was no precedent and partly because of the low priority given to passengers in comparison with coal and other freight. As passenger use of the Stockton & Darlington increased, by 1842 it seemed sensible to provide somewhere for them to wait and North Road station was built.

The station environment today with its recorded sounds of steaming engines and shrill whistles easily convinces the visitor that it is 1825 and that 'Locomotion' will be pulling in soon amid a cacophony of hissing pipes and belching smoke.

Not only is Stephenson's 'Locomotion' on display at the Museum but also a collection of other historic engines and associated rolling stock including the 'Derwent,' the oldest surviving locomotive manufactured at Darlington, built only a few yards from where she now stands.

Famous engines on display include the N.E.R. No

1463, (2-4-0) built in 1885 principally to haul the heaviest express passenger trains between London and Edinburgh. The 910 (2-4-0) is an express passenger loco built in 1875 to haul express passenger trains between York, Newcastle and Edinburgh.

Amongst the Museum's fascinating displays of rolling stock is an S & D coach from the 1840s which still shows many of the characteristics of horse drawn road coaches - just as Darby's iron bridge across the River Severn replicates the forms of carpentry.

To see period trains in a period station is an unusually rich experience. But the Museum not only features trains but also ticket offices, station kiosks, signs, posters, signaling lamps and all the paraphernalia of the railway worker, right down to a sample of his boots. There are many models and a large collection of books and illustrations for those with a more serious interest in railway history.

Gifts, souvenirs, railway books, postcards and posters are on sale in the Museum shop and drinks and confectionery are available at all times.

The Museum's special themed displays change annually and there is a temporary exhibition programme. Toy and train collectors fairs are also held at certain times of the year as well as a full special events programme.

A Stockton & Darlington Railway coach of 1846

Timothy Hackworth Railway Museum

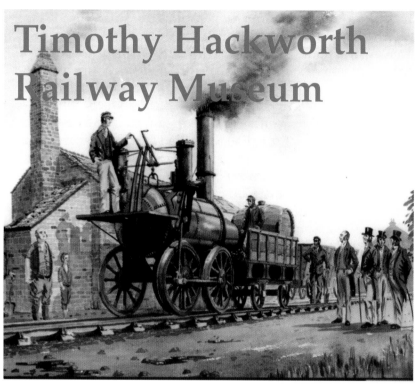

Timothy Hackworth's 1829 locomotive Sanspareil

Had it not been for the use of coal in iron making and the subsequent explosion in the use of iron for everything from tomb stones to factory buildings it is at least doubtful if railway development would have proceeded as early and as fast as it did.

Coal and iron were bulky and heavy and quite unsuitable for transportation by pack horse or even horse drawn wagon.

Indeed, it was this unsuitability, not to mention cost, which had led to the cutting of canals, the first, significantly, by the Duke of Bridgewater to carry his coals from Worsley to Manchester, where the price of coal was promptly halved.

Iron rails had been in use for some years at quarries,

mines, iron works and foundries around the country. The rails were flanged and the trains of trams or drams running on them were made entirely of wood and pulled by horses, after 1759, increasingly to link up with the nearest canal. As technology developed, the tram wheels became partly of wood and partly of iron until in the 1820s they became entirely iron, flanged and running along smooth wrought iron rails.

Steam pumps had been used to extract water from the tin and copper mines of Cornwall since as early as 1698 when Thomas Savery invented the first steam powered pump. In 1708, Thomas Newcomen invented a beam engine which drastically reduced the loss of energy inherent in Savery's device. But both engines were purely reciprocating and it was left to James Watt in 1783 to convert to-and-fro action into rotary movement.

The rotary steam engine was a universe away from a steam pump changing for ever the way people lived and worked. At first the new engines were stationary and housed in engine houses where they were used for winding but many a man dreamed of harnessing the new invention to traction.

One of the first to do so was Cornish mine engineer, Richard Trevithick who succeeded in building a locomotive in 1801. It was designed to run on the road but in 1804 he used a locomotive on rails to haul iron from Merthyr Tydfil to Abercynon in South Wales. Despite the brilliance of his invention, Trevithick's locos were too heavy for the rails they ran on. It was to be several more years before problems with engines and rails were fully ironed out.

Like most other developments of the Industrial Revolution, progress in locomotion can be seen to be very much a case of necessity leading to invention and of one man standing on another's shoulders to improve what had gone before.

Timothy Hackworth was a man cast in this mould.

Britain's North East, around Newcastle, is often described as the 'Cradle Of The Railways.' This was an area of coal mines and Hackworth, like Stephenson was from a mining background, both being born within five years of each other at the colliery district of Wylam, just west of Newcastle. A

Timothy Hackworth's 'Sanspareil' prepares for tests alongside other Stockton and Darlington locomotives in preparation for the historic Rainhill Trials at Liverpool in 1829

wagonway was used to haul coal from the colliery to the River Tyne.

Even as boys, Stephenson and Hackworth would both have known of the revolutionary power of steam. As young men, both would have been aware of Trevethick's experiments at Merthyr Tydfil and of his astonishing success in running one of his locos around a circle of iron rails at Torrington Square, London in 1808. The loco was called 'Catch Me Who Can' and those who dared did so. The idea did not catch on with the public but men like Stephenson and Hackworth were doubtless watching developments with interest.

Hackworth had been foreman blacksmith at Wylam Colliery and the services of himself and his men were much in

Timothy Hackworth

demand between 1811 and 1813 once the pit owners decided to introduce locomotives based on Trevethick's design - among them, the Wylam Dilly' and the 'Puffing Billy.'

George Stephenson was asked to amend the tramway survey to carry coal from Teesdale to the port of Stockton and, in the spirit of the times, he suggested the use of steam locomotives. When the railway opened in 1825, his 'Locomotion,' now in the Darlington Railway Centre and Museum, became the first loco to be owned by a public railway company. Dreams were being turned into reality at an unprecedented pace.

When Stephenson left the Stockton & Darlington to build the Liverpool and Manchester Railway, Hackworth was left in charge of Robert Stephenson's Newcastle works, where he was responsible for overseeing the building of 'Locomotion.' Hackworth was by now an engineer of growing repute, working in a field where the experts were still relatively few.

It was this experience that prompted Hackworth to sever his ties with Wylam and Newcastle for good and in May 1825 he arrived at Shildon where the new Stockton & Darlington Railway had its engineering headquarters. His appointment was as superintendent of engines and it was the window of opportunity he needed to move from tinkering to full blown locomotive design.

The man in charge of keeping the new engines running on a day-to-day basis bore immense responsibilities. When problems with this leading edge technology cropped up there was no one to turn to for advice other than Hackworth. But he was no mere problem solver; he was a leader who introduced important improvements to the steam locomotive.

Stephenson's first four locomotives performed poorly for the Stockton & Darlington. So much so that the company considered going back to using horse power. To save the day for the future of steam locomotion, Hackworth could see that what was needed was a new and more powerful engine and he decided to seize the opportunity to build a completely new engine under his own immediate control at Shildon. His 'Royal George.' built in 1827, became the most powerful then in existence and proved the supremacy of the locomotive over horse power.

Even by 1829, the jury was still out on locomotive steam power and assessment trails were set up at Rainhill. Hackworth entered his new 'Sanspareil' but the competition was won by Stephenson's 'Rocket' (now in the London Science Museum)

Timothy Hackworth's 1845 Derwent locomotive

earning Stephenson the title "Father Of The Locomotive." The 'Sanspareil' was heavy and heavy, too, on coke. There were also some mechanical problems which some thought might have been sabotage.

Despite this setback, Hackworth threw himself enthusiastically into loco design and manufacturing, becoming responsible for the creation of many of the Stockton & Darlington's locomotives. By 1833, Hackworth was strong enough to put himself on a non-exclusive private contractual basis with the Stockton & Darlington Railway. In 1836 he supplied Russia's first loco to the Tsar, and in 1838 he also supplied the first locomotive to run in Nova Scotia. By 1840 he had set up his own steam locomotive works at Shildon, the Soho Engine Works. His 'Sanspareil No 2' produced in 1849 was his last but its design would have been familiar even to school children of the 1940s, truly the forerunner of the most modern phase of steam locomotion. Understandably, Soho Works became famous as a training ground for locomotive engineers and mechanics and Shildon was one of the major railway engineering towns in Britain until the Wagon Works closed in 1984.

A replica of the 1829 'Sanspareil' can still be see in the Soho Engine Shed together with another of Hackworth's engines, the 'Braddyll.' The Engine Shed, on the original site of Soho Engine Works, where Hackworth's pioneering work was done, also contains many other important exhibits of the period including an 1830s beam engine used to drive machine tools. The underground hot air heating system used to dry newly painted locomotives is the only fully intact system of its kind in Europe. The nearby Shildon Goods Shed contains relics of the famous Stockton & Darlington Railway. Displays also show the key part railways played in the development of Victorian industrial towns. Vintage steam days are held in the Museum grounds throughout the year.

The importance of Timothy Hackworth and of Shildon will soon be recognized by an expansion of the Timothy Hackworth Railway Museum to be undertaken in association with the National Railway Museum at York.

To be known as Shildon Railway Village, the new visitor attraction in Shildon has been developed through a close partnership between the National Railway Museum in York and Sedgefield Borough Council. Both organizations are committed to the development of this landmark attraction which will bring a national railway collection to the North East and create a major new tourist attraction of national importance.

Costing £7.7 million and opening in 2004 the new building will display material from the National Railway Museum collection and will tell local, regional, national and international stories involving social and railway history.

The building's design will integrate its track side setting and proposals envisage a long, glazed frontage facing the Stockton and Darlington Railway that will make it appear as though Shildon's historic railway sidings have been recreated.

Hackworth lived, close to his men, at Shildon and his house is today the Timothy Hackworth Railway Museum. The collection illustrates the life and times not only of Timothy Hackworth and his family but of Shildon's railway community as well as Hackworth's unique contribution to the early development of railways. The new development will incorporate the existing Timothy Hackworth Museum and associated buildings.

For information about opening times and admission charges please contact:

**Timothy Hackworth Railway Museum,
Soho Cottages,
Hackworth Close,
Shildon,
County Durham, DL4 1PQ.
Tel/Fax: 01388 777999.
www.hackworthmuseum.co.uk**

Eden Hill

Val &
Douglas
Leeming

7, Linlithgow Road, Bo'ness,
West Lothian EH51 ODE.
Tel: 01506 822417
Situated in the town of Bo'ness, Eden Hill
is a family owned sandstone Victorian
house dating from 1880. It commands
outstanding views over the Firth of Forth
and is situated close to local amenities as
well as the preserved steam railway.
Bedrooms have either en suite or private
facilities as well as colour televisions and
complementary tea and coffee making
facilities. Private parking is available. No
smoking is permitted within Eden Hall.

Carriden House

Barbara and Graham Blackbourn welcome
you to their 16th century country home in
25 acres of park and woodland overlying the
River Forth, a mile east of Bo'ness Railway.
Full of history, the house occupies perhaps
the most ancient continually occupied
location in Scotland, the oldest recorded coal
mining in the country was undertaken within
the woods and the grounds host other
artefacts from over 2000 years of history.
Open all year, bed & breakfast in en-suite
rooms costs around £30 pp/pn.
Tel: 01506 829811
Fax: 01506 826888.
Email:
Carriden_House@compuserve.com
www.s-h-systems.co.uk/hotels/
carriden.html

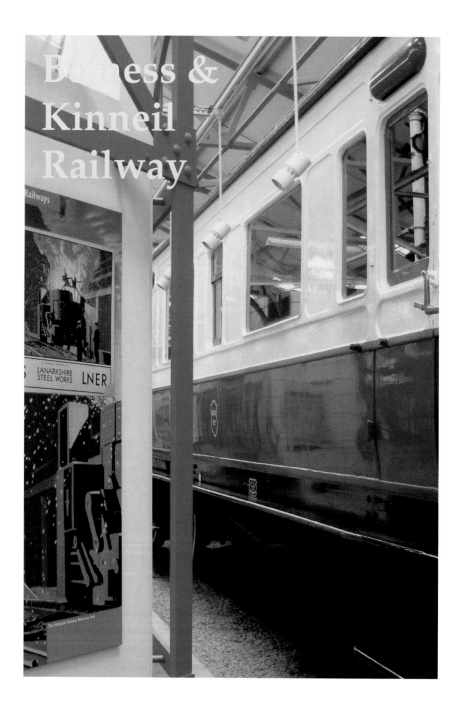

Bo'ness & Kinneil Railway

The Bo'ness & Kinneil Railway

A s everywhere, the railway in Scotland was the precursor of industrial change, while the availability of cheap travel transformed society. An additional role, of special Scottish significance, was to open up access for remote communities. A taste of the authentic character of railway development in Scotland can be had at Bo'ness, on the southern shore of the Firth of Forth.

Bo'ness is typical of small towns that have seen their industry decline and almost vanish. The town was once important for iron smelting and coal mining, and its harbour a base for whalers and later for an incoming traffic of pit props and the export of coal. There were iron foundries (one remains), a pottery, a distillery and a chemical works. The harbour was long the most significant on the upper Firth, until it was eclipsed by Grangemouth after the Forth & Clyde Canal to that place opened in 1790. Bo'ness Dock, and the Custom House, remain as testimony to a busy past. The dock and harbour were owned by the North British Railway, which developed them in connection with the railway.

Now Bo'ness Station is the terminus of the Bo'ness & Kinneil Railway, operated by the Scottish Railway Preservation Society. The railway recreates the branch line scene of the early or mid-20th century, and offers a 7-mile return trip from Bo'ness. Regular train services (every Saturday and Sunday from Easter until mid-October, and daily except Monday in July and August) enable visitors to see steam hauled trains in an authentic setting.

Bo'ness Station was built during the 1980s on cleared land adjacent to the town Dock. The advantage of an empty site was that the railway scene could be re-created using

buildings re-erected from elsewhere in Scotland.

Bo'ness Station train shed (the roof over the platform and tracks) dates from the dawn of the railway age, and was built in 1842 at the original Edinburgh terminus of the Edinburgh & Glasgow Railway, at Edinburgh Haymarket. The Edinburgh & Glasgow was the first line to connect two Scottish cities, and the Edinburgh station roof was typical of those being built elsewhere during the same early period - cast iron colonnades support arched beams at the wall head on which stand wrought iron roof trusses. The roof is of slates on wooden sarking. Here the cast iron work is decorated in a light classical style, and the result is a highly graceful building. Such structures were common at early major stations, but subsequent railway development and station enlargement swept all such away, except at Haymarket (and more famously at Bristol Temple Meads) where the later station extensions bypassed the original. Even when the lines through Haymarket were quadrupled (at the time of the opening of the Forth Bridge) the widened lines avoided the surviving station roof!

MODEST STATION

Beside the train shed stands a modest station building, of wooden construction, and typical of the economical habits of the North British Railway. This building was first erected at Wormit, located on the Tayport branch at its junction with the main line at the south end of the Tay Bridge, and was opened when the second Tay Bridge opened in 1887.

The signal box at the west end of the station was built by the Caledonian Railway in 1890, but stood on the line of the pioneering Monkland & Kirkintilloch Railway which opened in 1826 from the Monkland coalfield to the Forth & Clyde canal at Kirkintilloch. Part of the route north of Airdrie was utilised by the great Caledonian Railway's main line to the north. The Garnqueen South Junction where this signal box stood, marked the point where the main line left the original M&KR route at Glenboig. It is a typical Caledonian Railway design.

The Scottish
Railway Exhibition

Beyond Bo'ness Station, accessed over the station footbridge, is the large bulk of the Scottish Railway Exhibition building. The Exhibition presents a fine array of vehicles from the Scottish Railway Preservation Society's collection, which is necessarily a highlight of any visit to Bo'ness. There are on site 25 steam locomotives, 24 diesel locomotives, 72 carriages, 100 wagons and 3 steam cranes. These span over 100 years of railway development, and are representative of the Scottish railway scene. At any one time, some are in service on the railway, some on display in the Scottish Railway Exhibition, and unfortunately some have to be stored away in sheds and sidings.

In recent years, a major building programme has provided secure accommodation for most of the important items in the collection. The Exhibition provides the public access to collection items not in use on the operating railway. It contains six tracks on which Victorian locomotives compete for space with "modern" diesels, carriages demonstrate the high standard of Victorian main line comfort and a remarkable array of goods wagon types prove that railways really were the lifeblood of every industry.

In one part of the Exhibition this display of engineering variety becomes just a backdrop to fixed displays which represent different aspects of Scottish railways. "Making Scotland's Railways" shows how and why the system grew, "Running Scotland's Railways" shows how railways are operated, and how operations have changed over time. And "Using Scotland's Railways" present's the passenger's viewpoint. There is a working display of colour light signals, and a wealth of period photographs to illustrate each theme.

The Exhibition is completed by a conservation workshop, in which visitors can see items from the collection undergoing repair by volunteer staff.

James Watt and the Carron Ironworks

A journey on the Bo'ness & Kinneil Railway passes Kinneil House, on the western fringe of Bo'ness. (Although the railway runs through Kinneil, the house is best approached by road.) Here, between 1769 and 1773, James Watt worked on his improvements to the steam engine. The house was occupied by Dr. John Roebuck, an entrepreneur who was a co-founder of the Carron Iron Company, located just 10 miles away on the other side of Falkirk. The first furnace at Carron was blown in 1760, and the enterprise rapidly became a great commercial success. By 1764 additional coal supplies were required, and Roebuck took the lease of the Duke of Hamilton's coal mines at Kinneil. The mines were wet, and the Newcomen type of steam pumping engines which were installed were not up to the job. Roebuck entered into a partnership with Watt in 1768, and the latter worked in a small workshop adjacent to the house. The workshop now stands roofless, and beside it an engine cylinder casting (though it has not been linked with certainty with Watt). The experimental engine on which Watt worked at Kinneil was removed to Birmingham in 1773 when Dr. Roebuck met with serious financial difficulties and his interest in Watt's invention was bought out by Matthew Boulton.

The Birkhill Fireclay Mine

The passenger service on the B&KR terminates at Birkhill, three miles from Bo'ness, though the railway carries on for a further three miles to a junction with the Edinburgh and Glasgow main line. Birkhill is the site of an extensive series of mines, from which fireclay was extracted. This was an essential material for industry, made into bricks to line furnaces. Furnaces served many purposes - whether associated with steam boilers or with iron and steel making, refractory linings were essential.

Birkhill fireclay was a high quality product, high in alumina and therefore stable at elevated temperatures. It was formerly ground in a milling plant at the mine, before being loaded onto railway wagons for transport to Glenboig, near to Airdrie. There it was made into bricks for use in the furnaces of Central Scotland. Birkhill mine closed in 1980, when the number of customers for the product was rapidly shrinking.

Remarkably, local enterprise has kept the mine open to the public. From Birkhill Station, 80 steps descend alongside an old rope hutch haulage into the steep sided valley of the River Avon. Crossing the Avon by a bridge, the haulage emerges from the mouth of the most recently worked section of the Mine. The fireclay seam was 10 to 12 feet thick, and so the mine drift and the side passageways are tall. Worked on the traditional " stoop and room" system, a lot of fireclay remains in the stoops. Visitors are taken round the workings in guided tours, and can gain a little understanding of what underground conditions were like.

For opening times and admission charges please contact:

**Bo'ness Station,
Union Street,
Bo'ness,
West Lothian EH51 9AQ**

**Tel: 01506 822298
www.srps.org.uk**

Verdant Works
Dundee

West Henderson's Wynd,
Dundee DD1 5BT.
Tel: 01382 225282
Fax: 01382 221612
Email: admin@dundeeheritage.sol.co.uk
www.verdantworks.com

Open: Monday - Saturday, Easter to September 30
Wednesday - Sunday, October 1 - Easter

Whether goods were carried by sailing ships or steamers, the imagery of early industry in Britain very strongly includes foreign trade. And the fact that Britain became an imperial power is well known to be attributable to the growth of this trade to the point where Britain could think of itself as the workshop of the world.

Trade required ships and ships needed ports so around Britain's shores great docks grew up at cities like Bristol, Liverpool and Glasgow in the west and around the east coast, including London, at Hull, Newcastle and Dundee.

As trade grew, ships queued up to berth while work gangs loaded and unloaded the chests, barrels, bales and sacks of goods to and from quayside warehouses. Chests and barrels were made of wood but sacks and bales were made from jute, a plant growing mainly in the delta areas of the Ganges and Brahmaputra Rivers. There it was hand twisted and woven into a coarse cloth before being exported by the British East India Company.

MORE BAGS AND BALES

After the mid-18th century, industry and commerce grew together, linked by an ever improving transport system. The old empire of sugar, tobacco and slaves, based on a triangle including Britain, America and Africa was giving way to a new empire of manufactures. Everywhere men were experimenting to find new processes and techniques and the more successful they were the greater tended to be the growth in trade.

More and more bags and bales were needed and the East India Company was keen to export its jute. The problem was that jute proved difficult to spin because of its brittleness. Mill owners in Dundee already had experience of spinning flax, a blue flowered plant cultivated for its textile fibre and used in linen making. Jute was cheap and many linen products could be made from jute if only it could be machine spun. In Dundee and

Demonstrating the cop machine

elsewhere, there had been much experimentation and adaptation to produce machines capable of spinning brittle fibre. Jute was the most intractable of all.

Miraculously, technicians in Dundee discovered that whale oil, of which the town had a plentiful supply, was ideal for softening the jute fibres and making machine spinning possible. Jute spinning was begun in the early 1830s and within twenty years it had surpassed flax. At the industry's peak in 1900, 50,000 people in the city were employed in jute mills. Jute came to be used for sacking, tarpaulins, carpet and linoleum backing, roofing felts, tents and sand bags. Its appeal lay in its strength, low cost, durability and versatility.

Dundee was ideally placed to make the discovery that whale oil softened jut. Its whaling fleets brought home plenty of it. More importantly, a subsidy paid to encourage the manufacture of linen was removed so that other fibres, such as jute, became potentially more profitable. And an end to the stamping of linen cloth as a means of quality control also opened the doors to experimentation with other fibres. Flax was imported from the Baltic and continental war time blockades severely interrupted shipments and therefore production and profits. Dundee's merchants had rarely been in a more aggressive mood to try out new products.

The High Mill of Verdant Works was built in 1833 for David Lindsey, merchant and flax spinner. It is at the heart of one of the earliest urban industrial areas in Scotland. Mills grew up here from the 1790s onwards because of the availability of water to run the steam engines that powered their machinery. Like many Dundee flax mills in the 1840s and 1850s, Verdant Works switched to the more profitable processing of jute. By 1864, the Works is recorded as having three steam engines driving 70 power looms and 2,800 spindles. In comparison with 61 other textile works in the city at this time, Verdant's workforce ranked 16th in size. Verdant Works is a rare surviving example of a courtyard type mill, meriting its category 'A' listing as a building of national architectural importance.

MAINLY FEMALE WORKFORCE

The city of Dundee was an ideal home for the new industry because its entrepreneurs and workers already had long experience with flax. Being a port and ship building centre, it was strategically located to import the raw jute from India and even to build the fast ships needed to transport it.

Visitors to Verdant Mill today see little of the hot, noisy, greasy and dusty conditions in which the mainly female workforce toiled, often assisted by small children.

The From Fibre to Fabric Gallery

In 1883, out of 30,000 workers, about one fifth were under the age of 15 years. Children could work up to 19 hours a day and some fell asleep at their work. Machines could be placed closer together if they could be cleaned by small children. Today, school parties of all ages are welcome at Verdant Works, not to work but to learn about the past. There is an education suite where children can participate in pre-arranged activities.

Dundee became known as a woman's town and in the mills women outnumbered men by three to one. Perhaps the original of the 'house-husband' was invented here. Women had smaller hands and fingers and were often regarded as more diligent than the men.

Wage rates in the jute industry were among the lowest in Scotland and people worked long and exhausting hours. Many workers suffered from respiratory diseases such as bronchitis and many also became deaf.

For a child or young adult to be introduced to a lifetime's employment in a jute mill must have been depressing enough but home life was no picnic either.

Families were large with an average of eight people per two room tenement home even by 1911. Incomes were low, diets were poor and drinking water was polluted. Dundee had a serious problem with drunkenness as people drank to forget their misery and escape their problems. The mill women were no exception and binged as boisterously as any man. At home, while mothers gossiped, children played in the street. In the early 20th century, those who could afford it could go to a theatre cinema or dance hall.

The Mill office, open to visitors today, may have been the only oasis of tranquillity in the noisy Verdant Mill, its high desks and stools and large clock reeking of the 'masters' in a truly Dickensian way.

Today, the works is airy and well lit with displays, film shows, interactive computers and even some lovingly re-stored original machinesthat bring vividly to life conditions in the mill years ago and tell the fascinating story of Verdant Mill and even of Dundee itself with a plant growing far away on the Indian sub-continent. There is an excellent souvenir shop with a range of quality gifts, some even made from jute woven in the museum and there is a cafe serving refreshments from morning coffee to afternoon tea.

Right:
Weavers take a
break to pose
for a picture.

The Discovery

Discovery Point,
Discovery Quay,
Dundee DD1 4XA.
Tel: 01382 201245.
Fax: 01382 225891.
Email:
info@dundeeheritage.sol.co.uk
www.rrsdiscovery.com

Not far away from Verdant Mill is the Royal Research Ship 'Discovery', built in Dundee for the British National Antarctic Expedition of 1901-1904 and led by Captain Robert Falcon Scott. She was one of the last three-masted ships to be built in Britain and the first ship to be constructed specifically for scientific research and Antarctic exploration. At the turn of the 20th century, wooden shipbuilding was becoming obsolete and few yards were still capable of building strong, wooden-hulled ships. Dundee was the exception.

In the year 2000, RRS 'Discovery' was designated as one of the most important historic ships in the United Kingdom. At Discovery Point there are original historic objects, graphics, audio visual shows, models and dioramas, lighting and sound effects, interactive computer programmes and hands-on interactives. On a cold winter day, walking the decks, it is almost possible to imagine being in the Antarctic!

S team, coal and iron were the very basis of the Industrial Revolution, and of the three, coal and iron were rarely more cheaply to be found in Britain than in Scotland's central industrial belt, stretching from Glasgow and Edinburgh.

Iron was the principal material of the industrialization which swept Great Britain from circa 1760 to 1860 - iron bars and plates were the building blocks of the machinery, the bridges, the ships and the railways that made Britain the workshop of the world.

Iron-making needed coke for the blast furnaces and coke needed coal. To be viable, both coal and iron needed to be capable of inexpensive extraction, processing and shipment. Central Scotland possessed all these ingredients with the finest coals and blackband ironstone in abundance plus limestone, oil-shale and fireclay and the means by which to transport both it and the resulting products. Work on the Monkland Canal had been begun as early as 1773 to carry coals to Glasgow and the

Monkland to Kirkintilloch
Railway opened in 1826 - only
one year later than the famous
Stockton to Darlington line.
Soon, the areas canals and
railways formed a veritable
'spaghetti junction' of transport
networks serving the local iron
industries.

There was also a rich
source of labour as a result of
the 'clearances' in the Scottish
Highlands and the famines in
Ireland. In 1800, the landscape
of Central Scotland was
essentially rural but within a
generation it had been
transformed into a scene of
blazing furnaces and pounding
steam hammers. Centre to this
was the City of Glasgow,
which rapidly emerged as a
major centre of engineering,
shipbuilding, steam engine,
boiler-making and textile
machine manufacture.

Developments all made
possible by the readily and
cheaply available supplies of
iron and coal in its back yard.

The workforce, which
had flooded into the newly
industrialized Central belt of
Scotland, lived, for the most
part, in 'workers rows' of
single room terrace cottages in
the industrial towns such as

*A Coatbridge
ironworks at the height
of its activity, belching
out thick clouds of
black smoke and
lighting up the night
sky.*

Coatbridge or high-built and closely packed tenement housing in Glasgow. The results of industrialization were dramatic on the towns of Lanarkshire, for example, the population of Coatbridge rose from 740 people in 1831 (a year before the introduction of the 'hot-blast' iron-founding process) to 36,900 seventy years later.

In 1869, David Bremmer for the Scotsman newspaper described Coatbridge thus: "Dense clouds of smoke roll over it incessantly, and impart to all buildings a peculiarly dingy aspect. A coat of black dust overlies everything, and in a few hours the visitor finds his complexion considerably deteriorated by the flakes of soot which fill the air and settle on his face."

He continued: " To

experience Coatbridge it must be visited at night, when it presents a most extraordinary spectacle......from the steeple of the parish church the flames of no fewer than fifty blast furnaces may be seen......the flames have a positively fascinating effect. Now they shoot upwards and,

newspapers could be read by the light of the flames as they blazed forth from the furnaces.

The twenty-two acres of Summerlee Heritage Park lies at the heart of this bygone world of iron and coal, canals and railways - although no one could guess at its fiery past from its present air of tranquillity.

True to its heritage, the Park has been formed around the remains of the original Summerlee Ironworks and at the same time, shows something of the working and living conditions of those who once toiled in the local foundries and mines. The excavated site of the ironworks in the Park is virtually all that remains today of the proud tradition of the 19th century Scottish iron industry, which once included the great Carron Ironworks of Falkirk among its constituents.

The site of the Summerlee Ironworks was purchased in 1836 by John Neilson of Glasgow's Oakbank Engine Works. He was closely connected with the early history of the marine engine and with the use of iron in shipbuilding and he built the

breaking off short, expire among the smoke; again spreading outward, they curl over the lips of the furnace and dart through doorways, as if determined to annihilate the bounds within which they are confined." It is said that at night in Coatbridge, first iron steamship to sail on the River Clyde.

John was the father of James Beaumont Neilson, the inventor of iron-making's ' hot blast process'. He discovered that by blowing heated air into the blast-furnace to help smelt the iron, the result was increased output and reduced production costs. This, allied to the particular advantages of both central Scotland's coal and ironstone, gave the area a formidable industrial advantage.

By 1839, Summerlee had four furnaces in blast and by 1842, a time of general depression in the West of Scotland economy, this had risen to six. In the ensuing years, Summerlee iron was used to make everything from ships and trains through armaments and munitions to gutters, drainpipes, ornamental railings and even bandstands! The ironworks continued successfully until after the First World War, when following a brief boom period after the Armistice, increasingly scarce resources allied to industrial disputes at the mines, led to the furnaces being blown out in 1929. The ironworks were then demolished in 1938, although the workshops continued to be used for the maintenance of colliery machinery until 1950.

In the 1960s a new factory was built on the site to make hydraulic cranes and the main bays of this works form the present Exhibition Hall of the Park. Summerlee Heritage Trust was itself established in 1985, following the closure of the crane works, to preserve and display the industrial and social heritage of West Central Scotland.

While it is not a complete ironworks that today's visitor sees, the experience is closely related to the real thing. Inside the main Exhibition Hall a huge model shows what the works looked like in their hey-day. Just outside, the visitor can then oversee, from a raised esplanade the actual foundations of the original site with the bases of the blast-furnaces, blowing engine houses, boiler rooms and heating stoves all clearly visible.

Behind this view, and just by a restored branch of the Monklands Canal, from where canal boats once hauled the iron to Glasgow, is a recreated addit mine which aims to give visitors a realistic impression of the working conditions of a miner. This provides plenty of thrills - and chills - to visitors, especially those who have never been underground before. An addit mine is one that is cut into the ground, without the need for a vertical shaft, so (led by guides) visitors can walk down the slope to the 'working face' and experience the dark and cramped working conditions suffered by the men-folk, as they battled to win a day's pay for their families.

In conjunction with the mine is a row of miners' cottages, which show how miners' families lived, from the 1840s up to the relative comforts of the 1960s. In the 19th century, it was normal for families of eight to ten to live in these one-roomed cottages, with only a stand-pump in the lane for water and a communal earth closet for sanitation. Washing was done in a tin bath in front of the fire - father first and the rest followed, by order of seniority.

Summerlee has Scotland's only operational electric tramway, running over a half-kilometre of track. A 1910, open-topped Lanarkshire tram runs in fair weather, and more recent models from Glasgow and European towns provide covered transport at other times. Taking the tram back from the miners' cottages to the Exhibition Hall, the visitor can view extensive displays of working machinery, set out as if at a trade exposition or Empire Fair, of local industries, retail emporiums and social history. Opening for 2003 in an adjacent building is a steam-driven sawmill and exhibition on Scotland's timber industry.

Summerlee Heritage Park with its insightful and fascinating indoor and outdoor displays is indeed a monument to the Industrial Revolution in Scotland with all the more impact for being on an original site.

A fine selection of books and mementoes relating to the area's industrial heritage is available in the Summerlee shop, including a small book of poems by local poetess, Janet Hamilton (b. 1795), who summed up her local town as being: "Smorrin' wi' reek and blacken'd wi' soot". Changed are the days! Visitors can now picnic in the verdant grounds, or enjoy a snack or refreshment inside or outside the Summerlee tearoom as they plan their visit, or relax after an hour or two 'stepping back in time'.

Summerlee Heritage Park
Heritage Way,
Coatbridge ML5 1QD.
Tel: 01236 431261.
Fax: 01236 440429.
Website:
www.northlan.gov.uk

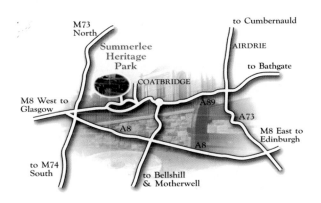

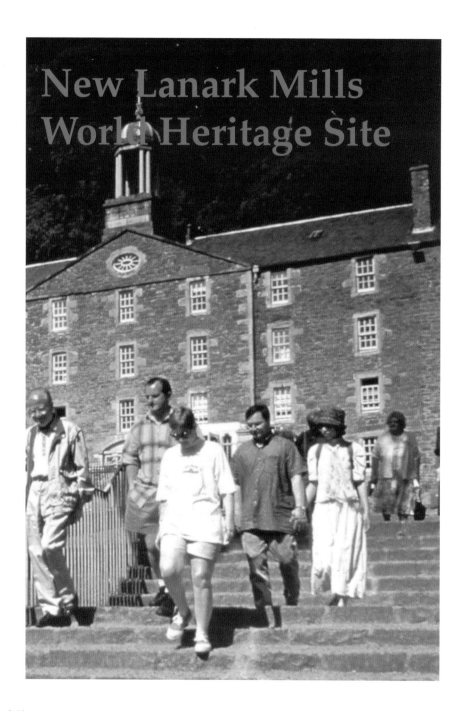

New Lanark Mills
World Heritage Site

The mill village of New Lanark is amazing even today and must have seemed unimaginably imposing when building commenced in 1785. The River Clyde at Bonnington Linn was a much painted beauty spot until a fateful day in 1784 when Glasgow banker and entrepreneur, David Dale, and his friend Richard Arkwright, the father of the factory system, visited the deep gorge and realized that the dramatic falls at Corra Linn from which the Clyde flowed on to Dundaff and Stonebyres made it the most "eligible situation for mills of all kinds."

The first of Boulton and Watt's steam engines was installed in 1783 but in Dale's day steam power had not yet become widespread in Britain's spinning mills. It was still raging torrents like those at the Falls of Clyde which the cotton masters favoured to turn the giant water wheels which drove their spinning machines. Impressed by the awesome flow of water, the two men began the construction of what were to become the largest spinning mills in Britain and the most famous cotton spinning community in the country and perhaps the world, so famous that today it is designated as a World Heritage Site.

Arkwright had already made a fortune at his mills in Cromford, Derbyshire, where his inventions had brought all aspects of spinning out of the traditional cottages and into some of the first factories Britons had seen. As at New Lanark, the mills dominate their surroundings like gigantic cathedrals of industry. At home and abroad the demand for textiles was rising and the market was so lucrative that entire communities were springing up on the back of its profits.

The son of a poor grocer from Stewarton in Ayrshire, Dale arrived in Glasgow at the age of 24 from an apprenticeship as a weaver in Paisley. In 1763 he set himself up as a textile merchant and 20 profitable years of business culminated in his appointment as first Glasgow agent for the Royal Bank. Within three years he had gone on to set up a turkey-red dyeworks at Dalmarnock and by 1785 the cotton mills at New Lanark. Cashing in on the profit from cotton spinning, Dale came to own five other mills in Scotland, often established in areas where unemployment was high.

Dale's entrepreneurial activities were by no means entirely motivated by profit - or, if they were, there were important incidental benefits for the community. Industry, employment and wealth were created in impoverished areas of Scotland, he established schools and he was a benefactor of Glasgow hospitals. It is important to know this because in an age of "dark satanic mills" and the sometimes cruel treatment and exploitation of workers, New Lanark would become famous for its owners' enlightened attitudes to employees.

Dale's partnership with the aging Arkwright did not last long but he continued building and by 1793 the clatter of water driven machinery daily breached the tranquillity of the beautiful area at the Falls of Clyde. The beauty of the site is gripping even today and it is no surprise that the area around the Falls of Clyde is a Wildlife Reserve.

But it is not only the natural surroundings which to this day are dramatically beautiful. The tall sandstone mills and tenements reflect classical industrial architecture, little changed from the period of the early Industrial Revolution. New Lanark is the subject of one of the most extensive restoration projects in Europe.

By 1793, thousands of spindles were at work in four huge mills, each up to 150 feet long and 30 feet wide. No 4 mill provided workshops, storage and dormitory accommodation for the workforce. The noise in the mill workrooms with their thousands of clattering spindles can well be imagined.

Throughout the 18th century population grew steadily but modern visitors are surprised to learn that out of 1,157 people employed in spinning in 1793, 800 were young boys and girls, often taken from orphanages. Of these, 450 were not even in their teens and included 95 nine-year-olds, 71 eight-year-olds, 33 seven-year-olds and five six-year-olds. It is small wonder that schooling occupied such an important place in the mind not only of David Dale but of New Lanark's most famous owner, the

A breathtaking view, looking down on the mills from the car park

social reformer, Robert Owen.

The use of child labour was normal in 18th century Britain and what contemporaries most remarked on was just how well treated the children of New Lanark were by the standards of the time. All this certainly did not amount to soft or cosseted living but the fact that only nine children died between 1792 and 1795 attests to high standards of hygiene and relative comfort when compared with the general squalor of the day.

The working day began at 6 am and ended at 7 pm - after which the children were expected to attend school for two hours. The only breaks were half an hour for breakfast and an hour for dinner. Breakfast consisted of as much porridge as they

could eat and dinner of barley
broth with "good fresh beef,"
cheese or, in season, herrings
and potatoes. By 1796, New
Lanark employed 16 teachers
who instructed over 500 pupils
in reading, writing and arith-
metic. In addition, two part
time teachers taught sewing
and church music. The day
school for under-sixes was
probably the first of its kind in
any factory community.

The dormitories at No 4
mill provided accommodation
for a fair proportion of the
village but as employment and
output expanded it was necessary to build more housing.
The earliest appear to have
been built near No 1 mill but
when unemployed migrants
from the Scottish Highlands
began to arrive, the elegantly
curved Caithness Row was
built for them. Long Row,
Double Row and Braxfield
Row were also added in the
1790s.

Although workers from
outside the village worked at
the mills there were clear
advantages to the early factory
masters to have their workers
on site. Most were from rural
environments and unused to
discipline. Factory owners

wanted hands who would be punctual and rarely miss work; on-site living made this possible.

Like David Dale, Robert Owen was attracted into cotton manufacturing and at the age of only 19 he was engaged as superintendent of a large spinning mill in Manchester employing 500 workers. Like Dale, Owen's father was a shopkeeper - a saddler and ironmonger. For a while after he left school he worked as an assistant in a draper's and grocer's shop next door to his home - he was only nine or 10. At the age of 10 he went to work for one of his elder brothers in London but after a short while became apprenticed to a draper in Stamford.

Lincolnshire. He had time to study and received a good business training. Next he moved to a draper's in London before joining the staff of a wholesale drapery in Manchester from which he was to move to take charge of Drinkwater's Bank Top Mill.

At Drinkwater's, Owen enhanced his management skills and even improved the product by being the first to use long-fibred American sea-island cotton. But Owen had realized that the key to success in cotton manufacture was not only the quality of the yarn but the quality of the workforce.

By the last years of the 18th century debate raged about what to do about an urban workforce that often lived in squalor and poverty and as often as not was intemperate and improvident. Some opined that lack of morality was the root of the problem, others that the cause was poverty. All agreed that something had to be done to improve the quality of Britain's workforce.

While he was not religious or a churchman, Owen believed that it was important to set workers a good moral example and to enforce morality by cracking down on such things as theft and drunkenness. He also believed, as David Dale had done, that management of a workforce, as well as setting the appropriate examples and exercising appropriate controls, was best done by employers providing on-site facilities, including housing and schools.

Owen was both a practical entrepreneur and a philosopher, not only concerned to improve working conditions as a means of enhancing production but as a means of increasing human happiness based on the fruits of production. His reputation as a manager was somewhat fearsome. Every aspect of his manufacturing operation was carefully regulated and supervised and his effectiveness was reflected in company profits.

Owen's management flair became widely known and he himself travelled widely throughout Britain's manufacturing districts, including Glasgow and New Lanark where he met and fell in love with David Dale's daughter, Caroline. By this time he had left Drinkwater's and entered into a business partnership which required trips to Glasgow. In 1799, Dale was 60 and thinking of retirement. When Owen and his associates made a bid for New Lanark, Dale accepted and with it a new husband for his daughter Caroline.

Owen continued and expanded Dale's policy of providing free schooling and added other facilities and services including a village store, a Sick Fund and free medical treatment, reminiscent of the later Welfare State. Owen was incensed by the scandalously overpriced and inferior goods sold to workers and was determined to both improve the quality of goods they bought as well as save them money.

The store, set up in 1813, was the inspiration of the modern co-operative movement and can be visited today, its shelves stocked as they would have been in the 1820s and 1930s. Of course saving his workers money kept demands for wage hikes at bay. New Lanark's 2000 workers were not paid outstandingly well but reasonable retail prices, low rents for accommodation and free services and amenities ensured that there was little discontent. Only one strike is recorded in the entire history of New Lanark and that a desultory affair during World War II which lasted only a few days.

Owen believed even more passionately than Dale that education was the key to eradicating poverty, sickness and criminality. He allowed no child under the age of 10 to work in his mills. His ambitious plans to build two large new educational buildings in 1809 provoked a bid by his partners to buy him out but Owen turned the tables on them and his plans went ahead.

His school aimed not only to inculcate basic skills but to widen horizons and to develop the full potential of his little community in a very modern way, teaching art, music, singing and dancing in addition to basic academic subjects. The school day was by no means all work and no play and sport and out-door recreation were encouraged. Mothers who wanted to work could leave their children at what was in essence a kindergarten and parents who themselves wanted to take advantage of the opportunity to improve themselves could attend evening classes at the Institute. Community kitchens were built in to make dining possible and the premises were used for concerts, dances and

Below: cotton workers around 1890

religious services. Owen was not pedantic about religion and there was tolerance of all beliefs.

Robert Owen's School is a major attraction for visitors today, especially the younger ones. It was within these walls that the system of infant education as we know it in Britain and much of the world began in 1816. By the end of that decade thousands of fascinated visitors had passed through Owen's schoolrooms and taken their impressions home to every part of Britain and beyond - to France and Germany, Switzerland and Austria, Russia and America. Modern visitors see areconstruction of a classroom of the 1820s and a dramatic audio-visual show in which the "ghost" of Annie McLeod, a 10-year-old mill girl tells about life in New Lanark at that time. There is also an interesting exhibition about the restoration of New Lanark.

Consistent with his educational ideas, New Lanark was a democratic place in which the community was encouraged to take responsibility for itself and even to learn the ways of democracy. The vote was not given even to men until 1832 and even then they had to be living in a property worth more than £10. Women had to wait almost another hundred years.

Residents' committees were responsible for what went on in their areas including even the dispensation of justice to any who were deemed to have behaved anti-socially.

Community rules included parents accepting full responsibility for the behaviour of their children, work for all able bodied people above the age of 10, temperance in the use of alcohol and being at home by 10 pm.

Owen's experience at New Lanark convinced him that he had been right in arguing that the way to efficient production and a harmonious community lay not in neglect and confrontation with workers but in looking after and developing them and making them a party to the enterprise for which they worked. These views led him to the concept of creating Villages of Cooperation "founded on the principle of united labour, expenditure and property, and equal privileges."

The villages were to be very much like New Lanark, self contained and clustered around a manufactory but set amid

A mill worker's house around 1820

gardens and allotments where workers could live healthy and moral lives. Owen became a staunch supporter of the trade union movement and some of his later ideas verged on socialism. At his Villages of Cooperation "the producer would have a fair and fixed proportion of all the wealth he creates." Owen took his ideas to America and many tried to emulate him at home and abroad but his lasting monument has remained New Lanark.

Owen's vision is perhaps best summed up by his remarks made at the opening of his Institute for the Formation of Character in 1816. He said: " I know that society may be formed so as the exist without crime, without poverty, with health greatly improved, with little if any misery, and with intelligence and happiness increased a hundred-fold, and no obstacle intervenes at this moment, except ignorance, to prevent such a state of society from becoming universal." His views had enormous impact on the course of social reform throughout the 19th century, especially education.

New Lanark closed in March, 1968 and fell on hard times. Its buildings succumbed to dereliction. The village population which had peaked at 2,500 in 1818 dwindled to around 80. It seemed that a great monument was about to die. Then in 1974 the New Lanark Conservation Trust was formed and the first steps taken on the long and hard road to restoring New Lanark and acquiring its designation as a World Heritage Site.

Today, many of the sandstone buildings have been fully restored and life has been returned to the village through the provision of modern rented and owner-occupied homes and the attraction of small businesses. Most of the housing is owned by a village association and is rented out to local people at affordable rents. One tenement has been preserved for posterity and some buildings, such as Robert Owen's House and the Millworkers' House, show how Owen and his family lived and how workers lived in the 1820s and 1930s.

An innovative Visitor Centre has been established in the Institute and Mill 3 where there are working textile machines and a fascinating audio-visual ride called The New Millennium Experience in which a young girl from the year 2200 named Harmony decides to delve into New Lanark's past assisted by riveting special effects.

Mill 1 has become the New Lanark Mill Hotel and a base for exploring Central and Southern Scotland. Wee Row has been converted into a Youth Hostel. Next to the hotel are luxurious self-catering 'Waterhouses' arched over the tail race of the mill on the River Clyde. As in the heyday of the mills, weddings and functions are now held at both the Institute and the hotel.

The centre of the site is dominated by the Mill Lade, the water channel built to lead water from the Clyde to water wheels in each mill. Hydro-electricity is still generated on site, from a 1930s water turbine.

An exciting programme of special events is held at New Lanark throughout the year; there is a spacious cafe, The Mill Pantry, for refreshments and in addition to craft products, books, gifts and souvenirs of a memorable visit there is a branch of Edinburgh Woollen Mill offering a wide range of knitwear,

Above: The mills before restoration.

casual wear and outdoor clothing.

New Lanark has gone from being a derelict industrial site to the winner of such accolades as the Europa Nostra Medal of Honour, the British Tourist Authority's coveted "Come to Britain" trophy and the Scottish Tourism Oscar for the best Visitor Centre of the decade - to mention but a few. New Lanark has refused to die, forging a new role for itself more than two centuries after it was created. David Dale and Robert Owen would have been well pleased.

**For opening times and admission charges please contact:
New Lanark Mills,
Lanark ML11 9DB.
Tel: 01555 661345.
Fax: 01555 665738
Email: trust@newlanark.org
www.newlanark.org
www.robert-owen.com**